UNREALISTIC
EXPECTATIONS

Unrealistic Expectations

BARBRA GOODYEAR MINAR

VICTOR BOOKS®

A DIVISION OF SCRIPTURE PRESS PUBLICATIONS INC.
USA CANADA ENGLAND

Library of Congress Cataloging-in-Publication Data

Minar, Barbra Goodyear.
  Unrealistic expectations: the thief of a woman's joy / by Barbra Goodyear Minar.
      p.   cm.
  Includes bibliographical references.
  ISBN 0-89693-542-6
  1. Women—Religious life. 2. Expectation (Psychology)—Religious aspects—Christianity. 3. Interpersonal relations—Religious aspects—Christianity. I. Title.
BV4527.M53 1990
248.8'43—dc20   90-32200
                                                                       CIP

2 3 4 5 6 7 8 9 10 Printing/Year 94 93 92

Contents

Dedicated to
the spiritually hungry

in memory of
Leone Hawkins Goodyear

Acknowledgments

Many fellow pilgrims have supported the writing of this book:

the writers of journals, articles, and books who wrote before me,

the speakers, singers, poets, and friends who inspired me,

and the lives of women who shared their stories with me.

I especially thank:

Carole Streeter, Afton Rorvik, and Victor Books for believing in the project;

Carol Lacy for editing and cheering me on;

Carolyn Johnson for listening and critiquing;

Pat Foxen for encouragement and proofreading;

Hazel Goodyear, Frances Walker, and Francie George for ideas;

my Bible study group for caring, solid prayers;

Ann Thornton and Rebecca Duncan for being my friends of the right hand;

my children Jeff, Katherine, and Steve for the wonder of their lives;

my husband Gary for his love and support.

Preface

During my life I have had many experiences common to women. I have dreamed dreams about how things *should* be and become impatient to make my dream life come true. Often, as I've walked through my earth days, I have been hit hard and knocked flat with a cold ocean wave of reality. Life is life—a mixture of happy moments, depressed hours, delightful days, lonely nights, weary weeks, good years, and tragic times.

In order to be in control and make things perfect, I used to manipulate myself and others. But life continued to have its own roller coaster ups and downs. How could I ever hope for any stability, peace, and joy?

The answer came when I changed my center from self to God.

It is a touch of this inward journey I humbly offer in this book. I write hoping to help you let go of unrealistic expectations, find freedom, and experience the rich treasure of Joy Himself.

Chapter One

WHO'S THE THIEF?
Understanding Unrealistic Expectations

Y ou guys knock off the fighting," I yelled at my eight-year-old Jeff and ten-year-old Steve. "Brothers are supposed to love each other, blast it all!" I pulled apart the tangle of wild arms and kicking tennis shoes. "Stop it right now!"

Some Easter vacation, I thought. I can't take much more of this. If it weren't raining, I'd throw them outside to run off some steam.

"I wanta do eggs," announced my four-year-old, scowling like an old woman. "Eggs now!" I heard the refrigerator door open and shut. No doubt about it. The eggs were coming out.

"Wait a minute, Katie." Turning to the boys, I narrowed my eyes. "Now you guys straighten up. It's Good Friday, and we're going to dye the eggs together. You each have a dozen—" I heard the eggs fall. Silence. Then a fierce wail filled the kitchen.

"They broke! They broke!" Katie bellowed.

"Oh, brother. Look what she did! Mom, look at this!" The boys were pointing and dancing wildly around Katie, glad to get the heat off themselves. To keep tennis shoes from stomping through egg yolks, I grabbed the roll of paper towels and got on my hands and knees. My preschooler found a sponge and stood on the edge of the mess, bawling.

At that moment my husband swung open the kitchen door. Home early. *Wonderful!* I thought. *He'll rescue me from all this.*

Gary tracked wet footprints up to my scrubbing spot and stopped to look. "Having a problem?" he asked.

"Oh, it's nothing," I snapped. "I'm just cleaning up two dozen eggs." He stepped over me and headed for the bedroom.

"Why don't you get the kids to clean up that mess? Where are my gym shorts? I've got a racquetball game."

"Still wet in the dryer," I said. He growled.

"I'll be home around 7."

"Give me a break!" I muttered, getting off my knees with soggy, yellow paper towels. I could feel my throat closing. I was furious.

The phone rang. Wiping my hands on my jeans, I jammed the receiver under my chin. Swallowing my anger, I said pleasantly, "Hello?"

Katie collapsed at my feet, crying, and the boys raced through the house. I strained to listen to the voice on the line.

"Oh, Mildred," I responded to her query. "I'm not sure I can be on the committee. Remember, we talked about this last week." As I listened to her next rush of words, my face flushed. Then I heard myself say sweetly, "OK—I guess I can help out."

I hung up, leaving the phone sticky with egg yolk. *I've got to sit down.* As I dragged into the den with Katie hanging on my leg, I caught my reflection in a wall mirror. *Horrible! If only I could lose this extra weight. If only I didn't have such a round face. I just hate it!*

I eased into my place on the worn, brown couch. Tears burned my eyes. I felt so disappointed. Deeply disappointed—with myself most of all, and also with my husband, my friends, and even my kids.

"Sorry, Mommy." Katie searched my face with round blue eyes and patted my limp arm with her pudgy little hand. I shifted her into my lap and felt her warm body snuggling against mine. How could I be disappointed in a four-year-old?

Later, shuffling wearily around the kitchen, I fixed the children a quick dinner and left them watching "Little House on the Prairie." The mother on the show was smiling. "Don't worry, Charles. I'll see to the farm. I'll take care of the cow, the children, and everything." It made me sick.

I stole up to our room, shut the door, and flopped across the double bed. The night rain poured down now, and I felt myself drowning in depression. It gripped me like a vulture. A black, familiar vulture. I hated it. I wanted to kill it. But time after time this kind of depression came over me and sucked the life out of me. *Why? Why am I in this mess? I'm supposed to be thinking about resurrection. But somehow I'm stuck in the Good Friday tomb.*

Stuffing my pillow under my aching head, I let my mind travel back through the afternoon. *Sure, it had been hard. But nobody had gotten sick and died. So why am I so depressed? So lonely—so empty?*

I had wanted to have such fun this vacation. I had a break from teaching, so I had planned picnics and movies and kite-flying, but with Katie's cold and the rain we were house-bound. I had wanted to be patient, but the kids got on my nerves, and I yelled.

Identifying the Thief

I wanted to wrap an apron around my spreading mother waist and bake chocolate chip cookies with the kids. But when I got everything out, they wanted to watch TV. I wanted to have family times and help the children focus on Jesus this Easter week. But Gary worked late or went to the gym. *Everything's fouled up. I'm not in control of anything. This horrible afternoon put a cap on a horrible week.*

Hot tears pushed against my eyelids. I let them come as I replayed the boys' fight in the living room.

It's not the fighting that hurts so much. It's deeper than that. They don't seem to love each other like brothers should. How am I supposed to teach them that kind of love?

The eggs were a mess. But I wish I hadn't lost my temper with Katie over a simple accident. And why did I let Mildred talk me into being on that stupid ways-and-means committee? I'm so mad at her!

No—I'm mad at myself!

But most of all I'm angry with Gary. How could he leave me like that? Couldn't he stop and save me from the mob of kids? For once!

The Depression Vulture dug his talons into my heart. But before I turned myself completely over to him, I choked out a prayer. "God, help me!"

I lay crying until there were more words: "I've been here so many times before. I feel happy and then I fall in this pit. Help me out of this depression. This heaviness. Don't let me go under this time. Please—God, rescue me. Love me."

I felt the Depression Vulture loosen his grip. The tightness in my chest eased. I lay quietly. Then something propelled me to think back over the afternoon. To look for a missing puzzle piece. The things that had happened were ordinary events. Why had they hurt so much?

Suddenly an idea dropped into my mind—the missing piece of the puzzle. *I'm disappointed because I expected. I expected my plans to flow without a hitch, even though they never do. I expected the kids to have fun with each other and with me. We were supposed to look like the perfect TV family, dyeing beautiful Easter eggs without a crack. Impossible!*

I expected my husband to sweep through the door, lift me from my knees, and announce he would never let me scrub the floor again— or at least be sympathetic and give up his racquetball game. Unlikely!

I expected Mildred to listen to the tone of my voice and not pressure me to help. Improbable!

I expected myself to look like a slim, oval-faced model like the ones I see in every advertisement. Ridiculous!

I expected! Over and over again I expected, and my expectations were constantly rained on. Why?

Pulling out my dust-covered Bible, I traveled through the pages. Then my eye landed on a verse that stood out like gold. "It was for freedom that Christ set us free; therefore keep standing firm and do not be subject again to a yoke of slavery" (Gal. 5:1).

The word *freedom* rang out in my mind. This was it! This was what I wanted. Freedom from slavery. But what was I a slave to? The kids? My husband? Mildred? Myself? Culture? Religion?

New questions were coming. I sat up in bed. *Could I be a slave to my expectations?*

I could hear the Depression Vulture whisper, "You're just making excuses. Expectations are good!"

I countered with, "But what about unrealistic expectations?"

Suddenly I knew I was a slave to unrealistic expectations. False expectations had stolen my joy. To make matters worse, this creeping thief was a creation of my own anticipations. Maybe I had tried too hard to make my dreams come true.

For the first time I felt excited. I knew God was guiding me past my depression into His truth. And I knew from His Word that the truth would set me free. I could have freedom—in Christ.

It seems that all my life I have wanted to be free and to be loved. (Can these two things coexist?) I have tried to find love by fulfilling the expectations of others—my parents and family, friends, teachers and preachers, my boyfriend, and later my husband and children, my culture, even myself. God expects a lot of me too. To be honest I expect a lot from others. How can I get out of the trap?

I could rebel against all the expectations. I would be free—but maybe unloved. Or I could be compliant—do what

I was told and fit in. I would give up freedom—but I would be loved.

I had chosen to be compliant.

I had given up my person to fill other's expectations. Now the burden of other's expectations piled on my back until I sagged like an overloaded, swaybacked donkey. I was caught. Imprisoned by unrealistic expectations. Who could set me free? Who could make me secure? Who would love me?

I knew the answer—God.

Maybe it was no accident that all this happened on Good Friday. Perhaps something could begin. to die here—tonight—so that my spirit could be resurrected in freedom and truth. If only I could let go of unrealistic expectations and replace them with God's expectations. *Lord, help me!*

Katie's little knock sounded on the door. "Mommy, can we dye now?"

I sighed.

"Daddy's home. He bought more eggs!"

Not what I expected. A surprise! And this time I would count my eggs *after* I had dyed them. I felt God smile.

Catching the Thief

Saturday morning the sun sliced through the clouds. I piled the cereal dishes in the sink and wiped up some sticky orange juice. As I grabbed the carton of cream for my second cup of coffee, I looked at the three dozen colored eggs stored in the refrigerator. The kitchen still smelled slightly of vinegar. My mind suddenly flooded with memories of last night—the depression—the prayer. Now who was this Thief the Lord helped me identify—the one who stole my freedom and my peace?

Oh, yes—False Expectations.

I could imagine Eve sitting in the perfect garden, her ear cocked to hear the tempting words of the whispering serpent. "If only," he promised, "if only you will eat the fruit from the tree of good and evil you will be like God."

My "if onlys" began dancing in my mind as I stirred my coffee. *If only I could eat of the fruit of the tree of good and evil, then I would have a happy life. If only my parents really loved me. . . . If only my friends understood me. . . . If only my teachers had appreciated me. . . . If only I were beautiful and healthy. . . . If only I could depend on the government to take care of my family. . . . If only my job were more fulfilling. . . . If only my husband could be more sensitive. . . . If only we had more money. . . . If only I could mold my children. . . . If only I could mother better. . . . If only I could meet the demands of the church. . . . If only I could be who I want to be. . . . If only God would come to me. . . .*

A knock broke into my thoughts. Marsha stuck her head through the back door. "Can I come in for a minute?" My young neighbor's voice cracked with emotion. Dark circles outlined her brown eyes. I poured coffee in her favorite yellow mug as she slumped into my wicker rocker, dropping her chin and letting her long brown hair almost cover her face. I waited. Finally she looked up.

"You know how I planned to go back to school this fall. Well, John told me last night that he wants me to put it off and work full-time. I'll never be anything without my education." Marsha wiped her eyes. "I just can't seem to get my life together. I work on one thing and something else falls apart." I reached for her hand.

"Marsha, I know how you wanted to go to school."

Her eyes brimmed with tears. She shrugged. "It seems like I keep living for other people. Keeping them happy. I'll disappoint my dad if I don't go to school and make John angry if I do. Sometimes I feel like I'm missing my own life!"

Marsha's comments haunted me long after she left. She felt she had lost power over her life. She was a victim. Everyone else's expectations pulled at her until she felt torn in all directions. If she couldn't shake free, the expectations would steal her life and she would never find peace.

I began to evaluate where I allowed others to dictate my life. How deep did the resentment run in my subconscious because I gave in to others' demands? Rarely did I resist those voices of authority that seemed to have permanent residence in my mind, telling me what I should or should not do. Was I missing my life by simply doing what I was told and never thinking about it?

Now that I knew a Thief was creeping around, I wanted to handcuff him and throw him out! But some serious barriers restrained me.

The first barrier was that I wanted my parents, teachers, friends, husband, children, culture, and church to be pleased with me. If they were all pleased with me, then I would feel loved and free to be happy. They would all jump in and fill up my emptiness. Knocking down the barrier of their expectations of me seemed impossible. I would risk losing their love.

Also, I wanted my parents, teachers, friends, husband, children, culture, and church to fill my needs. In my mind I judged, manipulated, and directed them to meet my expectations. If I gave up my control of them, I would never find my happiness.

Eve's temptation was mine. I also listened to the serpent whispering "what ifs" and "if onlys." It dawned on me that God's revelation to me on Good Friday meant hard work for the rest of my life. If I honestly wanted to get rid of false expectations and live in God's freedom, this Thief of unrealistic expectations must be barred forever from my life. Something far greater than daydreams, hopes, and wishes had to fill up my emptiness. I took the first step toward new freedom by recognizing the Thief. To go any farther I had to risk everything.

Jailing the Thief

That was it! I would risk it all. I would get rid of this crazy way of thinking and living. I would stop living according to others' expectations. And I would quit expecting others to meet my expectations. My mind swirled with excitement as I pulled out the flour to make pies for Easter Sunday. I would be the new Eve and jail the Thief. No more unrealistic expectations for me!

"Mom, I forgot to tell you. Grandma called yesterday when you were in the garage." Jeff stuck his finger in the flour and licked it. "Grandpa's sick and they're not coming for Easter."

"Stop that! Your hands are dirty." I heard the sharpness in my voice. "Why didn't you tell me sooner?" I felt the disappointment knock against my chest. "I'd better call them."

I phoned my stepmother and heard about my father's flu. Easter was a family tradition. My father always smoked a turkey. Hazel made her famous potato salad, and I made pecan pies. They drove over early so we could go to church together. After dinner the kids hid their Easter eggs and made their grandpa find them. This Easter they weren't coming. I felt my needy hole yawn open.

"Maybe I won't make these pies. We'll have ice cream." I shoved the pie tins back under the low cupboard.

If only they could come, I thought. *If only they could come, then I'd be happy. What a miserable week, and now this. At least Easter Sunday could have gone right.*

"Mom, aren't you going to bake the pies?" Jeff was still fiddling in the flour. "I like pecan pies." I looked at my eight-year-old's serious, freckled face. I was disappointed. My plans kept getting ruined. I didn't want to bake.

Suddenly I felt the footsteps of the Thief stomping around in my emotions, even though I had made a vow to banish false expectations from my life forever. I was tempted to hate myself for failing so soon, but I had a choice. This time I was not going to let depression steal my life.

"Grab those pie tins, Jeff. And get out the pecans!"

As we rolled out the dough, I found myself laughing and turning to the fun of the moment. I had almost given myself over to depression. But I didn't! It was evident that changing my way of thinking and reacting needed more than a simple vow. This was going to be WAR. After all, I had thought this way all my life. Like Marsha, I was living as a victim of forces outside of myself, letting them dictate my peace. I needed to change.

Being patient with myself is nearly impossible. After all, I live in a world of instant mashed potatoes, instant microwave dinners, instant TV solutions, instant news. I am part of an impatient people. Even the Christian church encourages me to read "how-to" books by well-meaning writers who tell me new ways of living in three easy steps. Then there are the "name it and claim it" believers who tell me that in Jesus everything is a quick fix.

Changing this way of living will take time, patience, and healing. I will run into suffering. According to the saints, I should embrace suffering's lessons. This time a quick fix is impossible. The small lesson concerning the pecan pies showed me the need for personal decisions to live different-ly—one tiny step at a time.

I thought of my Good Friday verse: *"It was for freedom that Christ set us free; therefore keep standing firm."* I want that free-dom! I want to be free of this Thief.

Where can I start? Maybe I could inventory my losses. When was I first robbed? How did it happen?

As I lay in bed that night, with the Easter baskets and the Sunday-best clothes ready for the morning, my prayer came out on a sigh. "Lord, set me free."

Then, I sensed God trying to break through my thinking. He vividly reminded me of the three days of darkness Jesus spent in the tomb. His frightening death was only the begin-ning—the beginning of new life. Perhaps my darkness was the beginning of something—if I was ready for life.

Restoring Freedom

Easter morning. Heavy rain pelted the windows. I woke up empty. I reached across the bed, longing for a touch from my husband, but Gary was already up. I knew he was reading the Sunday paper. I lay in bed and heard the children downstairs digging into their Easter baskets. I wanted them to run upstairs in their excitement and hug me and tell me they loved me. But they were eating jelly beans and looking for eggs. *I should teach them more of the meaning of Easter and give them less candy. How can I feel unhappy? I haven't even started my day.* I felt the Depression Vulture flapping his wings around me.

I wish my folks were coming today. It won't be the same having Easter dinner alone. Such a disappointment. Oh, well. Get up and get going. No expectations, remember. Resign yourself and go on.

My emptiness grew deeper. I pulled myself out of bed and found the blue dress I planned to wear. *If only I could lose five pounds, it wouldn't pull at the waist. If only we had the money, I could have a new dress.* I shot a look in the bathroom mirror. *If only my face weren't so round.*

We made it to church. The place was packed. Katie broke the elastic band under her chin that kept her lacy hat in place. I took the hat away from her and held it in my lap.

"Be still, Steven," I said, jerking his arm. "Here, you sit by your dad. Don't eat those jelly beans in church." With a pasted-on smile I tried to manage the kids. I only hoped I could get through the service. I felt like crying.

Easter. The highest holiday of the Christian faith. The celebration of life over death. I felt swallowed by depression as I sat among the Easter people, absorbed in my personal darkness.

Suddenly I stopped to listen to my own thoughts. *Here I am—listening to the "if onlys" of that sneaking Thief. If only they would hug me. . . . If only he would touch me. . . . If only they had come. I want my husband, children, parents to fill up that deep hole. Fill up my loneliness. And if they can't, maybe money or looks could.*

At least I was being honest, and the truth put me on the edge of light. The service went on around me, but I bowed my head. I listened.

Here was the risen Christ. Here to set me free from depression and death. Only He could fill me. I could exchange my unrealistic expectations—the Thief of His joy—for life in Him. I only needed to let Him work with me. Would I accept His gentle discipline? Would I let Him love me?

Yes!

I raised my head and said with the Easter people:

> *He has risen*
> *He has risen indeed!*
> *He is lifting me into life with Him.*

Thinking It Through

As you discover your own unrealistic expectations, I suggest you do some journal writing. Writing helps us work with our thoughts.

1. What are the "if onlys" in your life?
2. Who and what do you depend on to make you happy?
3. How do you disappoint yourself? Are you realistic in what you expect of yourself?
4. When was the last time someone let you down? How did you feel?
5. When was the last time you counted on an event to bring you happiness, and that event didn't meet your expectation?
6. How do you resolve your depression when you are disappointed?
7. Have you sincerely started your personal journey with God?
8. Do you believe that life with Him can bring you joy? How?

"And now, little children, abide in Him"

(1 John 2:28).

Chapter Two

CAN'T YOU FIX MY HURTS?
Unrealistic Expectations of Parents

I watched a young couple in the Country Clinic the other morning as they waited for the doctor. Their red-faced baby was squalling.

"Allen, hand me the blanket," said the mother, fussing over her squirming infant. "Maybe Jamie's feet are cold."

"How about putting on these things?" asked the father, pulling tiny yellow booties out of the new diaper bag. They put the booties on Jamie's tiny feet, changed her diaper, and snuggled her into a navy blue carrier on her father's chest. The child settled down.

I was glad to see these parents working hard to satisfy their child's needs. It was good for her. The bonding and care will help establish her security. But even doing their best, eventually these parents will fail Jamie. It is impossible for them to meet all her needs.

I'm Your Kid—Love Me!
As dependent children, we turn to our parents. Their job is to provide physical and emotional security and to help us build our sense of self. That's a big order. None of us had perfect parents, so we all have experienced a less than per-

fect parent-child relationship that left us with internal needs.

When I directed a large preschool and kindergarten, I watched children trying to squeeze their parents into meeting their needs. Their manipulations often wrung the hearts of parents who wanted to make their children happy.

One year, on the first day of school, I circulated through the rooms, checking on the teachers and children. In the four-year-old room I spied sullen faced John clinging to his mother. Moving quietly toward him, I bent down. He grabbed at his mom's leg with both hands and howled mournfully. His long cry and forlorn look announced big trouble.

His mother looked at me with equally forlorn green eyes and stroked her son's perspiring blond head.

"John, let's go play with the children." I spoke softly. "Mommy will be back soon. Right after we have juice and crackers." I hoped the mention of snack time would work its usual magic. John pinched up his face and screamed. I suggested to his mother that she stay with him for a few days until he adjusted.

The next week we tried it again. When Mom started to leave, John threw a fit. This went on for three weeks. John and I were coming down to a duel. I sat on the floor beside him.

"Johnny, can you tell me what's the matter?" I asked.

John grabbed the edge of his mother's skirt and began to twist it. Finally he burst into tears. "I want her to fix my hurts!" Once John could express his feelings he began adjusting to school. But his words stuck with me.

Daddy, Mommy, Come Help Me!

Deep inside we all want our parents to fix our hurts. After all, they brought us into the world. From the beginning they fed us when we were hungry, changed us when we were wet, held us when we hurt, rocked us when we were afraid. Many of us grow up expecting our parents always to fix our hurts, meet our needs, and fill up the gaping hole in our inner being. When we run up against something that is impossible for our parents to fix, we are shocked.

Of course, some parents try to fix everything and end up stunting their offspring's development. If John's mother had never separated from John, he would be unable to develop normally. Often, I saw a mother insisting that she button her child's coat or carry his school papers when the child was quite capable of doing these tasks himself.

Smothering a child's independence with overattention is another example of the Thief at work. The child begins to expect the parent to do everything for him. Still, when a healthy parent-child break takes place, it can be frightening. The child feels that empty hole.

When I was three years old, the kitchen screen door snapped shut, cutting off the tip of my index finger. I remember vividly the blood and the panic of getting to my mother. "Mommy, help!" I screamed, holding my finger in the air. "Mommy, help!"

My mother did what she could. Soothed me. Promptly got me to the doctor's office. But she had to turn over the problem to someone else. The next time I got hurt I asked her to take me to Dr. Smallwood. I had begun to learn that Mother could not fix everything.

My friend Sara tells this story:

When I was five, I climbed a tree beside our house in Ohio. I'd been eyeing that tree for quite a while. I practiced getting a toehold in the rough trunk and grabbing a low limb. One Saturday afternoon I swung my leg over the low limb and climbed up into the tree. I can remember the exquisite feeling of accomplishment. After a few minutes of joy, I hoisted myself up on the next branch and then the next.

Dad watched from the front door. "Daddy, come see me!" I yelled.

"That's fine," he said. "Better climb down now."

I froze. Climb down! Climbing up was one thing. Climbing down another.

"Daddy, come get me! Come help me!" He went inside. I couldn't believe it. I clung to the tree crying. My daddy left me. He wanted to teach me that I could take care of myself, but I didn't understand.

I don't remember the climb down. I do remember feeling abandoned by my father. A few months later he left for Army duty during World War II. That was the ultimate abandonment.

No doubt about it. All children have stories like these. We have unrealistic expectations of our parents. We are deeply disappointed when they fail to fill up our empty hole with love and understanding.

If we have a secure home which is full of love, we are fortunate indeed. Our empty hole will be at least partially filled. It is through this love we gain some understanding of the Holy Parent who invites us to call Him Abba Father, Daddy.

In his book *Help! I'm a Parent,* Dr. Bruce Narramore says:

My experience in counseling neurotic adults has invariably shown that their image of God has been colored by negative experience with parents, God's representatives on earth.[1]

When we wonder if God really loves us, if He really understands us, if He is angry and wants to punish us, if He sees us, if He really has a plan of good for our lives, if we can depend on Him, then we are reflecting the experiences we received from our parents and authority figures.

When Jesus said, "Let the little children come to Me," He knew what we needed (Matt. 19:14, NIV). All of us are little children. We need to come to the perfect Life-giver— the Parent who longs to fill us and who can fill us. Our Abba. Our Daddy.

Please, Meet My Needs!

Each year as preschool director I gave our school families a publication from the National Association for Mental Health on the needs of children. The publication lists the obvious needs of good food, plenty of sleep, and exercise. Then it goes on to list eight basic emotional needs—needs that, if they are not met for a child, can lead to death.

- *Love:* Every child needs to feel that his parents love, want, and enjoy him; that he matters deeply to someone; that there is someone who will care for him.
- *Acceptance:* Every child needs to believe that his parents like him for himself, just the way he is, all the time, not only when he performs in a certain way; that they separate who he is from what he does; that they can help him grow and develop in his own way.
- *Security:* Every child needs to know that his home is safe and good, and that his parents will be there for him, especially if there is an emergency; that he belongs to the family and has a place in that family.
- *Protection:* Every child needs to feel that his parents will keep him safe; they will save him from the strange, the unknown, and the frightening.
- *Independence:* Every child needs to know that his parents will encourage him to grow up and experience new things; that they believe he can succeed in doing new things.
- *Faith:* Every child needs to live by a set of moral standards and believe in the finest human values of honesty, sharing, courage, and justice. [I believe every child needs to be taught about God our Father, His Son, Christ Jesus, and the Counselor, the Holy Spirit.]
- *Guidance:* Every child needs to have help in learning how to act toward people and things and to have help from people who care about him. He needs adult models who demonstrate how to respond to every situation.

• *Control:* Every child needs to know his limits. He
needs his parents to hold him to these limits. He needs
to understand his feelings of anger and jealousy. At the
same time he must not be allowed to hurt others or
himself because of these feelings.[2]

Often children can deal with many physical hardships if
they have the emotional love they need. But Helen wasn't
that lucky.

Even at sixty-three the pain of her childhood flooded Hel-
en's face as she told me the story of her life in Virginia. It
was a story of abject poverty—lack of decent food and housing, and abandonment by her father.

"The fourth grade was the hardest. That was the year I
learned that Daddy had a girlfriend. My grades dropped. It
seemed like one day I could do math, and the next day I
couldn't understand it."

This was the first time she remembered experiencing depression. The family's poverty frightened her. But she de-
fended her father. "I always thought Daddy loved me even
if he didn't come home much. My mother constantly said,
'Be a good girl.' I tried as hard as I could to be good and
compliant, so I wouldn't burden my mother and so Daddy
might come home.

"I had a long road to health. I needed deep inner healing.
A Christian counselor told me about God, who longed to be
my Father. Now I know I'm wanted, and He will never
abandon me."

Every child is born with legitimate physical and emotional
needs. Despite Herculean effort, no parent can ever give a
child a *perfect* love relationship. Only God as Parent can give
tailor-made, perfect, individual love, because He is God, our
Creator. David writes about this Father God in the Psalms:

O Lord, Thou hast searched me and known me.
Thou dost know when I sit down and when I rise up;
Thou dost understand my thought from afar.

Thou dost scrutinize my path and my lying down,
And art intimately acquainted with all my ways.
Even before there is a word on my tongue,
Behold, O Lord, Thou dost know it all.
Thou hast enclosed me behind and before,
And laid Thy hand upon me.
Such knowledge is too wonderful for me;
It is too high, I cannot attain to it (Ps. 139:1-6).

Stay Close to Me

The birth pains are close together. The mother bears down hard and pushes. The father coaches the mother to breathe. A final push and the baby emerges. The infant starts breathing on her own. The doctor ties and severs the umbilical cord. The baby is placed on her mother's chest. Now, separated from that warm, protected oneness she experienced within her mother, the baby begins her life journey.

Perhaps some of our yearning for oneness comes from our experience with the woman who housed us in her womb. We reach out looking for the oneness again. When it eludes us, we experience a brokenness. We sense an aching loneliness.

The baby seeks affection and signs that she is connected to someone who serves as parent. There is a well-known experience documented in a Brazilian orphanage where children had all their physical needs met. They had good food, plenty of sleep and exercise, but the orphanage lacked enough staff to give the babies affection and love. They were alone. Most children died within their first twelve months.[3]

The mother is the soil from which the baby nourishes herself. But in the process of developing, the baby begins to draw away from Mother in separateness. The process is like a teeter-totter. Baby runs from Mother, laughing all the way, and then rushes back and grabs her legs. During this mysterious play between mother and child, the child exercises separation.

M. Scott Peck, M.D. writes in *The Road Less Traveled:*

With experience the child begins to experience itself—
namely, as an entity separate from the rest of the world.
When it is hungry, mother doesn't always appear to
feed it. When it is playful, mother doesn't always want
to play. The child then has the experience of its wishes
not being its mother's command. A sense of the "me"
begins to develop.[4]

But what if the mother-infant interaction is grossly disturbed? Then the child works even harder to get his needs
met—or gives up and dies.

Julie stared at her lap as she told her story. "When I was
eighteen months old, my mother was taken to a sanatorium
to recover from TB. I stayed with my aunt. After eight
months Mother came home, but I kept my distance and for a
few months I wouldn't speak.

"Finally, one day at lunch I looked around the table and
said, 'I've been gone.' My parents thought my comment was
darling, but it meant more than they knew. I never really
trusted my mother to be there for me again." Julie looked up
and smiled sadly. "I got the idea that if I could be real good,
I'd be safe somehow. The rest of my childhood I lived in my
own fantasy world and was hostile toward the adult intruders
I couldn't trust."

Clearly, Julie missed having her security needs met, and
she felt an aching loneliness. But Julie's story continues. "I
remember in the third grade that every Sunday I walked to
church with Mother. That year I began to have a knowing of
God. He was real and He was big—big enough to keep my
world together. After that I was always searching for God.
My desire for Him never ended." Julie's emptiness began to
fill when she got in touch with her Holy Father—a Parent
who would never leave her.

Recently I heard of the ultimate rejection by a parent.
Lisa's early history vibrated with pain. "I never knew my

father. He left before I was born and died before I could find him. I never felt secure with my mother, but I didn't know why." Lisa's eyes grew red. "I have to say like the song, 'I looked for love in all the wrong places.' I really made a mess of my life. Then two years ago my mother told me she had tried to abort me. I was shocked and brokenhearted. No wonder I never felt wanted."

Few of Lisa's childhood needs were met. When she was thirty-two, Lisa met the Abba Father and started a healing journey into Love.

Don't Hurt Me!

No matter how our parents, grandparents, aunts and uncles might have tried, we all have deep needs that have gone unmet. Wars, moves, divorce, unemployment, illnesses, births of new siblings, and deaths come as a part of life, robbing us of love and security. These are events that affect everyone. Some children have experienced even more trauma—physical, sexual and/or emotional abuse.

It is difficult for those of us who have had a somewhat normal life to understand what it's like to live with emotional or physical abuse as a child—and how deep and black the need-hole becomes.

Five-year-old Cindy and her mother lived with Cindy's grandmother. They moved into her small apartment because Cindy's mother was trying to kick her cocaine habit. Cindy got up for breakfast one morning with two black eyes.

"Oh, baby, what happened to you?" asked her grandmother, holding the tiny girl in her arms. She feared Cindy's answer.

"I fell off my bed—two times." She looked straight at her grandmother.

"You know that's not true." Now Grandmother was crying.

"Did Mommy tell you? Don't be too mad, Gram-mommy. She's so sick."

Cindy protected her mother. Even after all the abuse, she hoped Mother would fill up the emptiness. If she could only be good enough.

Cindy's bruised eyes told others of her suffering, but often children carry no external signs of their internal agony. Their private hell is kept secret. When the child grows up, the injured "child within" continues to bleed from the wounds of abuse until healing comes.

One morning Vicki showed me her wounds.

"Vicki! Gee, I'm glad to see you," I said, opening the back door for my friend's beautiful, college-age daughter. Vicki paused before coming in. Then in slow motion, she walked to the kitchen table and slumped down in a chair. I handed her a mug of hot chocolate and waited. We had talked together many times over her growing up years, but I was unprepared for this conversation.

"I feel safe with you. I have to tell someone." Her tears broke free. "My father—my father . . . " Little by little the story emerged. Vicki had been sexually abused by her father from the time she was four until she was sixteen. She kept the abuse a deep secret. My heart broke realizing she had lived alone in her tragic silence.

That night she dared to walk into truth. Through intensive help, Vicki is being set free of her past. She is letting the perfect Father love and heal her.

Continue to Parent Me

As we grow up, our need for affection still runs deep. We long for connection even though we struggle toward independence. We try to ward off the isolation we feel. We want to be interdependent—reconnected.

We still hear a voice, influencing our whole person. The voice that dictates direction and self-image is often the voice of our parents. Even if our parents live far away, or even if they have died, their powerful voices judge us and instruct us. Beth's story illustrates such power.

As soon as Dr. Macky's funeral ended, I searched outside the large downtown Methodist church for Beth. Finally, I caught a glimpse of her auburn hair shining in the morning sun. Working my way through the crowd, I reached my childhood friend.

"I'm so sorry about your dad," I said, squeezing her hand.

"I'll miss him so." Her voice fell to a whisper. "But I'm free."

For a long time Beth's words haunted me. I knew Dr. Macky's death had set her free in a sense. I'm sure he loved his daughter. But his fathering had sent an unspoken message with it: "Live up to my expectations, and I will love you." Over the years Beth had lived her life to please her father, but because of his perfectionism, she had never quite made the mark.

Would Beth really be free now? Probably not. His words and attitude could live inside her head and color her life to the end unless she had some deep healing. She needed to know she was loved not for her *doing* but for her *being*. That is the gift her Father God has for her.

I was blessed to have a loving, concerned mother. We were close. When she died unexpectedly at age forty-six, I felt totally empty. My agony of loneliness was beyond anything I could stand. I searched through the house for something that would fill up my need. I smelled her clothes. I kept scraps of paper that contained her handwriting. I felt angry. I knew, intellectually, she would die sometime. Everyone died. But somewhere inside I never expected it to happen. Death was the ultimate abandonment. My mother had left me.

I had been raised in the church, but it was this great need of parent, that aching empty hole, that propelled me into accepting the parenthood of God. My own Abba Father. In my aching hunger I began an honest new search for someone who would never disappoint me. One who would never leave me. One who would love me. I found Him.

I clung to His words. "For I will turn their mourning into

joy, and will comfort them, and give them joy for their sorrow. . . . And My people shall be satisfied with My goodness" (Jer. 31:13-14). As I leaned into God, a real magnificent Power who loved me, my empty hole began to be filled—by letting Him pour into me.

I experienced God's filling me in all sorts of ways, collectively through all sorts of people. Through my Uncle Dave who held me close at the funeral. Through my father who began sharing his feelings for the first time. Through my friend Sally who had lost her mother and understood. Through Mrs. Morris who had lost a daughter and extended her love to me, an orphaned young woman. And eventually through my stepmother Hazel who lovingly grandmothered my children.

I didn't expect parent love to come from any of these people. I didn't demand or manipulate or rebel to fill my needs. But I was open—open to the surprises God my Father had for me.

Learn to Forgive Failure

Where do we begin?

We have legitimate needs that our parents for whatever reasons never filled. All of us have wounds and scars that remain in the child within us.

Some of us are still driven by the voices of our parents or other family members. We may still manipulate by compliance or rebellion, trying to make our parents give us what we need. We may give in to our parents' manipulation. All this—to break into the isolation and loneliness we feel.

Dr. Hugh Missildine describes the memories we carry as the "inner child of the past."[5] He believes this "child" tries to control how we live by listening to the positive and negative parenting voices of the past. We must take time to evaluate our attitudes. Are we living out our lives from what *we* believe or what our parents told us to believe?

The Lord challenges us to think with Him saying, "Come

now, and let us reason together" (Isa. 1:18). If we listen to His parenting voice, He will guide us from the hurting voices of our past into health and freedom.

The Lord tells us to forgive our parents. Forgiving our parents for their failure in meeting our needs as a child is a golden key to our health. Yes, it may be important to understand how and why our parents failed us. But understanding is not forgiveness and healing.

Beth started her process of forgiving after learning that her father came from an alcoholic family and was driven to perfectionism.

My friend Helen understood that her mother did her best to feed and clothe her. She came to understand that her father was suffering from deep childhood hurt of his own when he left her family. Still, only when she began forgiving her parents for the hurt they had inflicted on her, did the heaviness lift.

Little Cindy may be defending her mother now, trying to understand that she is sick. But in order for Cindy to become healthy, she must be willing to forgive her mother's gross abuse.

I understood that my mother couldn't live forever, but I had to forgive her for dying and leaving me all alone.

We all expected our parents to love and care for us. We expected them to be there when we needed them. We wanted them to be perfect. These expectations were unrealistic. Here are some ways parents hurt us:

• *Parents may hurt us with good intentions.* They may overprotect us and smother us with their involvement. They may try to mold us into the child they want.

• *Parents may hurt us because they are out of control.* They may be the victims of drug or alcohol abuse, divorce, or physical and mental diseases. As their children, we become victims of these things too.

• *Parents may hurt us because of their own personal mistakes and problems.* Our parents have had broken parents too. They are in need of forgiveness and healing as much as we

are. They make mistakes because they are human and looking for love and security. As their children, we often suffer
from feeling responsible for our parents' unhappiness.

How can we forgive our parents for those things that happened to us as children—those things that made us distrust-
ful, disturbed, and hungry for love?

Forgiving the hurts from our parents will take time. The
first step is to see the need for forgiveness, and the second
step is to make the choice to forgive them. I was motivated
to learn how to forgive when I realized that the forgiveness I
offered another was for my own healing. When I understood
this, I got serious about those I needed to forgive.

In his book, *Forgive and Forget: Healing the Hurts We Don't
Deserve*, Lewis B. Smedes says there are four stages of forgiveness. The first stage is hurt. The next stage is hate. The
third stage is healing. And the fourth stage is trying to come
together with the party you need to forgive. (Sometimes this
is impossible and you have to be healed alone.)⁶

In order to move through the stages, we can begin with
penetrating questions.

● Ask yourself: "Do I want to be a whole, healthy person?
How have my parents knowingly or unknowingly failed me?
Am I willing to forgive them for my own sake?"

● Tell God: "Help me to forgive my parents for
_____ (be specific here). I am will-
ing to be released from the anger and hurt I carry because of
them."

● Be patient. Forgiveness and healing take time. Each
time you feel trapped by emotion from the past, make an
offering of forgiveness again.

● Don't expect to forget. I believe that an abused child
never forgets the abuse, but after forgiveness and healing,
she can let go of hatred and anger.

The Lord instructs us in Matthew to forgive up to seventy
times seven. Why? Because forgiveness brings *us* health and
peace. Once we can forgive the sins of our parents against
us, once we can begin to see that our heavenly Parent loves

us differently from our earthly parent, we can fill our lonely, needy heart, our empty hole, with His love.

Lisa is now full of peace and purpose. I asked her how she ever recovered after finding out her mother tried to abort her.

"I carried on in my hurt and anger until I couldn't stand it anymore," she said. "I went to counseling for several years. Finally, I listened to what I prayed—almost absentmindedly in the Lord's Prayer: 'And forgive us our debts, as we also have forgiven our debtors.' I knew I needed to forgive my mother. So I began asking God to help me.

"For a long time I would flood with depression or anger when I thought about IT. But finally the feelings stopped coming up. Yes, it was a fact of my life, but I had no more emotion about the attempted abortion.

"It seemed I was more open to God being my Parent. The Parent who wanted me. Let me read you this from Psalm 139.

For Thou didst form my inward parts;
Thou didst weave me in my mother's womb.
I will give thanks to Thee, for I am fearfully and won-
derfully made;
Wonderful are Thy works,
And my soul knows it very well (Psalm 139:13-15).

"You see," she looked at me and smiled, "He wanted me."

I could see! Lisa had let her Abba Father fill up her aching void, and together they were making a healthy, beautiful life. She was letting the perfect Parent parent her. Lisa had realistic expectations of her God.

Thinking It Through

1. What expectations do you have of your mother?
2. How has your mother failed to meet your needs?

3. When did you specifically need her, and she didn't come through?
4. What have you done with all the hurt?
5. Are any of your expectations of your mother unrealistic? What are they?
6. What expectations do you have of your father?
7. How has your father failed to meet your need?
8. When did you specifically need him, and he failed to come through?
9. What have you done with all the hurt?
10. Are any of your expectations of your father unrealistic? What are they?
11. Are you ready to forgive your parents for your own sake?
12. Can you accept God as your Perfect Parent?
13. What promises does God make to you as His child?

"See how great a love the Father has bestowed upon us, that we should be called children of God; and such we are"
                                                    (1 John 3:1).

Chapter Three

WON'T SOMEBODY LOVE ME?
*Unrealistic Expectations
of Friends*

I was hanging up my little, red wool coat with the real, brown leather buttons in the cloakroom of Mrs. Johnson's prekindergarten when I saw Heather hiding under some jackets. She wore a yellow scarf over her head and tied in a knot under her chin.

"Come on, Heather. Let's play," I said. Heather was popular, and I wanted her friendship.

"I can't." She rubbed big tears away with her tiny fists. "Mama cut off my hair." I remember taking her by the hand and leading her out of the jackets.

"Let me see." I tugged off the scarf and stared at Heather's shorn head.

"I wish my mama would let me cut off my hair," I said, knowing in my five-year-old heart that I would die if I lost my long blond braids. I had lied—not really to make Heather feel better, but to make Heather like me.

My friendship with Heather taught me that if I was nice to a person and flattered her, she would be my friend. It was a long while before I learned that I was being manipulative to fill my need. I was too young to know that I wanted Heather's friendship because I needed security and self-esteem.

37

Two Are Better Than One

"The Lord God said, 'It is not good for man to be alone' "
(Gen. 2:18). How well we know it. How deeply we feel it.
We need connections with other human beings. We long for
that one person who will understand and take us in, the one
who will know us and still love us. Unless we find a friend
who will take us in, we will be isolated and abandoned even
if we have possessions, talents, and beauty.

Once we leave the bosom of our family, we begin to reach
out to people beyond. Even as young children we long to be
accepted. At first, toddlers play side by side almost oblivious
of their peers. Gradually, however, they become aware and
involved with one another. Three-year-olds begin to play
together, and four-year-olds are into the social scene. Best
friends and group cliques appear and "who is in" and "who
is out" often change from day to day.

With preschoolers we can observe friendship-making in
the raw. Children need friends. They want to be popular.
Young children gifted with beauty, intelligence, and wealth
usually develop strong self-esteems and have more power
than other children. They don't mince words and often use
their power ruthlessly.

Betsy, one of my little students, told her mother she was
never coming back to preschool. Her mother called me for a
conference.

"What seems to be the problem?" I asked. I had observed
that Betsy was cantankerous.

"Betsy says no matter what she does the children don't
like her." Betsy's mother rubbed her hands in her lap. "I
feel so sorry for her. She cries about being left out."

"Do you have any thoughts about what's going on?" I
asked.

"I know she tries to make the children do what she wants.
She's pretty bossy."

"I think Betsy is lonely. She wants to make friends, but
she doesn't know how. What if we work on some friendship
training?"

Even at four, in her great need to have friends, Betsy was forming unrealistic expectations about friendship. She wanted, she demanded, that other children fill up her lonely spot. And if they failed, Betsy often hit them. With a lot of patience on the part of her teacher, her mother, and the other children, she began learning about being a friend. One thing Betsy started learning was that a friend added to her life but could not take away all her lonely feelings.

As we extend our need for acceptance beyond our parents, we turn to our peers. Beginning attempts at friendship may go well for some, but for most of us these attempts are riddled with low points and disappointments until we learn how to let go of unrealistic expectations. We must learn that, as much as we try to manipulate them, our friends can never fill all our needs.

Hopefully, in our infancy and early childhood our parents gave us physical and emotional security and encouraged our self-esteem through acceptance of our person. As our individuality emerged, between ages four and five, we began taking over this internal role ourselves.

Finding belongingness through relationships comes more easily to the child whose early needs were met. Children who feel insecure grow into adults who feel insecure and have unrealistic expectations of others. That's because they try to gain the safety and acceptance they so desperately need through their relationships.

Who will accept me? We rejoice when we hear God say, "I have loved you with an everlasting love; therefore I have drawn you with loving-kindness" (Jer. 31:3). We go to Him and let Him be our security. We go to Him and let Him show us who we are. Then we will not try to extract our security and self-esteem from other people.

Linda came from a low income family in Ohio. She was the third daughter in a family of five children. Through hard work, her mother kept the family going, but her role model locked Linda in a box.

"I can remember desperately wanting friends as a child. I

was so lonely. But we were terribly poor, and I was embarrassed by my clothes and our poverty. I think, though, I couldn't make friends because of my mother. She wasn't a communicating person. She didn't have friends. She didn't reach out for help even though sometimes we went without food. She had fierce, fierce pride.

"She kept our hand-me-down clothes starched and ironed. When we went out we were to advertise a certain way. You didn't wear your grief outside. Nobody was to know your business. It was punishable by death if you told anything from home.

"I was shunned as a girl by the other children. It broke my hungry heart. But I can see now that I gave others messages too: 'I can never let you know who I am,' and 'I need more than you can possibly give me.'

"I think I began to break out of this after I heard that there was a God who knew all about me and still loved me. At first it was hard to believe. Little by little I began risking my real self with others."

Linda began to draw the basic security needs from a God she could trust. She learned that He accepted her and that she was precious in His sight. Then, because these basic needs were met, she began to have realistic expectations of friends. People could help meet her "belonging" needs in life, but they could never be the spring from which she drank for self-esteem and security. Only a relationship with God could provide that.

Friend-A-Mania

Probably junior high and high school are the most difficult time for friendships. Teens base their security on how many phone calls they get each night. They begin to look alike, talk alike, and think alike. Teens seem to group themselves into such categories as socials, jocks, druggies, actors, musicians, and egg-heads. They find it hard to cross over from group to group, merging personal boundaries.

Friends are everything. As adolescents detach themselves from their families, they throw themselves into friendships. Friends help give them their identities. They don't know themselves without each other. They live by the old saying:

We aren't who we think we are.
We aren't who others think we are.
We are who we *think* others think we are.

"Jenny was my best friend in eighth grade," explained Carol. "I remember we spent every Saturday night together at her house or mine. We shared all our secrets. When my period started, I told Jenny before I told my mother. Jenny was my life. I thought we'd be best friends forever.

"We daydreamed about boys and called them on the phone. But then Jenny started going steady with Bobby. I was terribly jealous of him. Bobby stole my best friend." Carol shook her head. "It was a horrible time for me, and I was depressed for weeks. Our friendship was never the same."

Carol tried to fill her inner hole with Jenny. When Jenny moved on to another relationship, Carol was left painfully empty. As adults, our relationships grow more sophisticated, but this kind of situation with friends tends to repeat itself— if we are trying to fill our internal needs through people.

"I'm glad I'm graduating," said Lynn. "Even though I've made some good friends in high school, so much of the friendship scene has been painful. I learned something from a horrible experience as a freshman." Lynn looked at me with round brown eyes. "I ran around with a snippy bunch of girls, and someone in the group was always on the outs. Whoever was the victim was the center of gossip and meanness for a week or two. I was pretty good at keeping everybody happy, so I avoided the 'third degree' until the end of the year. I never thought it would happen, but the group finally turned on me.

"Thank goodness I had faith in God. Those two terrible

weeks I really prayed—and listened. I think it was the first time I let God love me. When the girls wanted to make up, I was glad. Friendships are deeply important to me, but since that experience I haven't let friends take God's place."

Lynn learned early what many of us still need to learn. As important as they are, friends are only one part of our lives.

Clearly, when we are free from trying to manipulate others to give us our sense of self, we are liberated to really love. We can stop trying to make others fill up our empty hole. We realize that it is our responsibility to take care of our inner needs with God. We let go of unrealistic expectations of others and set them free. We can embrace Paul's words: "But let each one examine his own work, and then he will have reason for boasting in regard to himself alone, and not in regard to another. For each one shall bear his own load" (Gal. 6:4).

When we let go of unrealistic expectations, we can then enjoy our relationships and let them develop—exploring and learning about each other in a healthy way. We begin to pay attention to what we can give each other—with no strings attached.

Friend Addictions

I believe that some of us get into relationship addictions because we want so much to be known and loved. In her book *Co-Dependence: Misunderstood-Mistreated*, Anne Wilson Schaef writes,

> Co-dependents are relationship addicts who frequently use a relationship in the same way drunks use alcohol: to get a 'fix.' . . . People who are so completely externally referenced will do almost anything to be in a relationship, regardless of how awful the relationship is. Co-dependents have no concept of a self that others could relate to; whatever small vestige of the self does exist is easily given away in order to maintain a relation-

ship because they feel like literally nothing without the relationship.'

We who come to know ourselves through God let go of these addictions and establish friendships in freedom.

Extroverted, fun, intelligent Sandy is a young mother in her thirties. In Bible study we were discussing having unrealistic expectations of others. "I've always had one friend at a time," she said. "I want my friend to know everything I feel and think, to go places and do things with me. I guess I really want to suck her into me." She dropped her head. "Maybe that's why each one finally left the friendship."

Sandy was addicted to her friends. The friendship she offered had a hook. And the people she caught were expected to fill Sandy's great need of knowing and accepting herself. Now Sandy is learning to give love freely, giving up her secret agenda of control. She's beginning to seek the friendship of the Holy Friend and learn who she is—and how much she is loved.

Jesus loved His friends. He was the ultimate lover, yet He often went away by Himself to be with His Father. He made it clear that His joy was completed by knowing the love of God the Father.

Love Songs versus Reality

I was in the seventh grade. The cold Christmas wind whipped the green pine wreath as I opened the door wide for Jimmy. With blushing face and shaking hands, he handed me a small tissue-wrapped box tied with red ribbon.

"Merry Christmas," was all he could choke out before he fled on his bike. I bubbled up a "Thank you!" before shutting the door. I remember bouncing up and down on the couch as I ripped open the package. A small rooster pin lay on a tiny slice of cotton in a Newberry's Dime Store box. It's red jeweled eye peered at me. This was love. Jimmy was my prince. How could I be so lucky? I phoned all my friends and bragged about my conquest.

By the time Christmas vacation ended, Jimmy was riding his bike to my friend Susan's house. I was a devastated has-been. The Depression Vulture circled over my head.

Like every girl, I dreamed of romantic love, of my prince that would come and love me. As I grew older, my dreams grew deeper. Some man would appear—probably from across a crowded room. We would merge together, become one. He would know me. Protect me. Cherish me. Together we would make our own world. "The Sound of Music" scenes played in my head. I was Maria Von Trapp. Like Maria, my joy would be perfected—through a man. To say the least, my expectations of romantic love were unrealistic.

Often we single-mindedly search for a mate. We want to "fall in love" because then we will be filled up with joy. Our loneliness will end; we will absorb and be absorbed by another. We'll have no personal boundaries between us. This is the love myth. Many people move from relationship to relationship when their love fails to live up to this myth.

"I think my friends and I have been in love with the idea of love," said Lynn. "And so many of my high school friends are having sex because they think they can make their boyfriends commit to loving them forever. I'm really glad I've stayed a virgin. I can see that the girls who give themselves sexually to a guy don't keep the guy 'in love' with them.

"My mom told me that no matter how much I wanted to be a part of another person, our skin would always separate us." Lynn is learning that she must be whole inside. We can never draw our personal wholeness from another individual.

Dependent Lovers

M. Scott Peck, M.D. describes dependent people searching for love:

> They are like starving people, scrounging wherever they can for food, and with no food of their own to give

to others. It is as if within them they have an inner emptiness, a bottomless pit crying out to be filled but which can never be completely filled. They never feel "full-filled" or have a sense of completeness. They always feel "a part of me is missing." Because of their lack of wholeness they have no real sense of identity, and they define themselves solely by their relationships.[2]

Jeannie is an attractive brunette who has had two marriages and, after recently ending an affair, is now in counseling. We talked one afternoon about her choices. "Ending my affair with Scott has been really painful. I thought I loved him," said Jeannie. "But I realize now I was trying to use him. I had no idea how to be friends with Scott, much less his true lover. I needed him, just like the other men in my life, to rescue me from a domineering mother and abusive father.

"Here I am in my forties still trying to get someone to love the little girl inside me. I've got to let go of my fantasies about men and solve some of my own problems."

In our search for love, we continue to drink from other people unless we begin to grow spiritually. This was the problem of the woman at the well. Jesus knew her need and gave her the answer to her thirst for love. He said, "But whoever drinks of the water that I shall give him shall never thirst; but the water that I shall give him shall become in him a well of water springing up to eternal life" (John 4:14).

We, who learn to remain in Him and drink from His love, learn what true love is. We learn who we are and how to give ourselves away. We learn that without Him we cannot truly love. In Him we will have joy.

The Art of Making Friends

As we open ourselves up to God's love for us, we can begin to give and receive the gift of friendship. Understanding the stages of friendship can help us become better friends, lovers, and eventually, marriage partners. Knowing what to expect, we can ward off the Thief of our joy—Unrealistic Expectations.

● *Phase one is the meeting period.* We meet someone and begin to "feel him or her out." We find our new friend interests us. Perhaps he or she fascinates us. We explore the other. Our relationship solidifies.

● *Phase two brings maturity.* Together we commit to being friends. We increase our relationship. Then we hit truth. It's at this point that many people drop the relationship. The myth of perfect friend/perfect lover falls apart. This person who has enchanted us also disappoints us. Many people detach themselves at this point and look for a new relationship.

● *Phase three challenges the relationship.* We struggle through rough times. We bargain. We end the relationship or we recommit ourselves to it. Friends who have gone through struggles together have the rare gift of a friend who walks in when others walk out.

One of the greatest friendship experiences of my life has been with a group of five women who met every Thursday for seven years. Our backgrounds were varied. One of us lived in great wealth; one of us struggled out of the welfare system. Three of us finished college, one (probably the most intelligent) finished high school at the age of thirty-five. There is more than a twenty-year spread in our ages. Collectively we have experienced singleness, marriage, divorce, remarriage, and widowhood.

We learned to be fast friends. The Lord was the center of this group. He was our source of love and our personal security. He came to us through the encouragement, honesty, commitment, and affection of one another. We argued together, ate together, cried together, laughed together, shared thoughts together, and prayed together. We trusted each other, and our trust was rewarded. Best of all we were free to be who we were and who we were becoming in Christ.

Our group is now a twosome because three of us relocated, but there is still a oneness of five. I have come a long way from my childhood manipulation of always being "good" to have friends. With these friends I am able to practice honesty and, to my surprise, I am still loved. No, better yet, I am loved even more for my humanness.

After we accept the responsibility for the security and self-esteem needs within ourselves, we are ready for healthy friendships and loveships.

Dr. Alan Loy McGinnis gives some helpful insights to making and keeping healthy friendships in his book *The Friendship Factor.*[3]

To make friends:
- Assign top priority to your relationships.
- Cultivate transparency.
- Dare to talk about your affections.
- Learn the gestures of love.
- Create space in your relationships.

To cultivate intimacy:
- Use your body to demonstrate warmth.
- Be liberal with praise.
- Schedule leisurely breaks for conversation.
- Learn to listen.
- Talk freely about your feelings.

We can see from this list that love is more than feeling. Love is action—the action of letting go and loving freely.

During my devastating first love experience with Jimmy in the seventh grade, my wise mother gave me this advice. "Pretend your friends are like a ball of mercury that you hold in the palm of your hand. If you try to grip the mercury, it will break apart and squeeze out between your fingers. But if you leave your palm wide open, it will remain there." So I try to remember to work at loving my friends in freedom—with my palm open wide.

Choosing to Forgive

We hold unrealistic expectations of family, friends, and loved ones. We want them to love us perfectly. We want them to take away our loneliness and give us self-worth—to be God for us. We want them to know us, and in that knowing, merge with us.

Friends are people. People are human. Humans fail. So we can expect that our friends and loved ones will let us down and disappoint us. Sometimes they will even turn on us, abandon us, and betray us. Jesus experienced the ultimate rejection of a friend when one of His closest, chosen confidants betrayed Him to His death.

Here again we are called to forgive—for our own spiritual peace and health.

When I was in college, a Jewish political science professor told our class with great bitterness about his imprisonment by the Nazis. "I was turned over to the Germans by a so-called friend," he said, running his hand through wiry, gray hair. "Now I trust no one."

My heart ached for him. He had gone through an excruciating ordeal, and he could not let go. If he could forgive, he could start his journey to freedom. He was still trapped in his torture. It was his agonizing unforgiveness that helped me determine to let go of some resentment of my own.

I had a friend who had deeply hurt me. The memory of what had happened between Judith and me would often flare up. I kept thinking she would apologize. When I thought about the incident, an acid bitterness would burn in my mind. By willing myself to forgive, I put to rest the false expectations I had of my friend. Through God's help I thrust a mortal wound into the Thief of my joy. I began to experience freedom as I walked in that forgiveness, and I began to experience the meaning of these words: "Therefore, if anyone is in Christ, he is a new creation; the old has gone, the new has come!" (2 Cor. 5:17, NIV)

Remember that forgiveness is an act of the will. Many people confuse the act of forgiveness with a change of emotion. They believe that if they still feel some hurt or anger, they cannot forgive. Changes of emotional feelings come after we choose to forgive. Forgiveness is a matter of intent.

Friendship is giving—as well as receiving. We cannot give out of an empty place, and we cannot give love for the purpose of being filled. John tells us, "We love, because He first loved us" (1 John 4:19). To be healthy friends and lovers, we must attend to our spiritual life. When we let God's love pour into us, we can pour love out to others because we are full.

Thinking It Through

1. During your childhood what did you learn about making and keeping friends?
2. How did you try to get people to like you?
3. What did you do when you felt left out and hurt?
4. As a teenager, how did you manage your friendships?
5. How did you manage to stay in "the group"?
6. Did you ever manipulate your friends? How?
7. When and how did you place your security in your peers?
8. As an adult, how do your friends disappoint you?
9. Are you realistic about what you expect from your friends and your relationships?
10. Do you have unrealistic expectations in your male-female relationships? What are they?
11. How can you separate your fantasies from reality?
12. How can you set your male and female friends free from your unrealistic expectations?
13. How can you strengthen the relationships with your friends?
14. Are you ready to ask God to fill you with His love? How can you pour that love out to your friends?

"We love, because He first loved us"

(1 John 4:19).

Chapter Four

WHO AM I SUPPOSED TO BE?
Unrealistic Expectations of Self

The summer afternoon steamed. I picked up the stack of magazines I'd been saving, kicked off my sandals, and curled up in front of the fan. I opened the June issue of a slick-covered magazine and skimmed the table of contents: "Is Your Hair a Flop?" "A Psychic Changed My Life"; "Fanny Fitness: How to Get Your Bottom in Top Shape"; "Are You an Excitement Junkie?" Sighing, I let the first magazine drop to the floor and opened a Christian magazine. *This would be more like it,* I thought. "Fifteen Ways to Be a Better Mother"; "How to Serve Your Church"; "Are You Pleasing Your Husband?" I watched droplets of water form and run down the sides of my tall glass of iced tea like giant tears.

I exploded with thought. *Who am I supposed to be? No matter what I read or where I look, someone is telling me how to lose weight, what to do with my face, what I should cook, how I should raise my kids, how to live as a single, divorced, or married person, how to stay busy, how to deal with stress, or how to find God.* The Depression Vulture flapped so close I could feel the wind from his wings.

Wiping the sweat off my glass, I put it against my hot cheek, letting the cold burn my face. *I've got to get a hold of myself. I know that I'm always tempted to get moody in June—I love my birthday, but I always get these "my life is running out! Who am I supposed to be?" thoughts. Brother!*

Maybe I should go back to school. Certainly this year I've got to really get into the exercise routine. I flipped through the pages of a fashion magazine. *And my clothes need revamping. If only I could squeeze my budget.*

Wait—what am I thinking? I'm so selfish! Here I sit with a new outfit in the closet, a refrigerator full from yesterday's shopping, and I'm plotting for more? My life is only a wink in time.

I pinched the extra flesh under my chin that had dropped from nowhere. *I don't have much longer if I'm going to do something. I've got to pull myself together. I need to work on everything—body, mind, and spirit!*

I opened our church's newsletter. *What I need is to give more. Give my things away—give myself away. Serve the church. Make God proud of me.* In a frenzy I began reading the minister's column, "How to Discipline Yourself."

A putrid smell hit my senses as I felt the Depression Vulture land in my emotions. My mind swirled with expectations of myself. How could I be both a modern woman of my culture and God's woman? So many other voices were shouting directions.

Who am I supposed to be?

Let *Me* Tell You

Everyone needs to belong, to feel worthwhile, and to feel capable. Often we set up unreachable standards for ourselves. These excessive standards can knock us flat. We are insecure about our belongingness. We wonder if we are worthwhile. We overextend ourselves to prove we are capable.

One place we begin collecting unrealistic standards is our family of origin. The way we interpret what went on between ourselves and family members is the key. The old tapes echoing in our minds color our expectations of ourselves.

Linda is a workaholic. She worries about being worthwhile and capable. She is discovering why as she begins to untangle how she interpreted her childhood.

"When I was young, my mom hauled me to piano lessons, dancing lessons, and Brownie meetings," said Linda. "She even selected my clothes and suggested who I should be friends with. I know she meant well, but I remember hating the routine! I felt so pressured." Linda shook her dark head slightly as she thought about it.

"Somehow I got the idea that just being me wasn't enough. I had to be MORE than me. I tried to add to myself by what I wore, who I knew, and what I did. I really lost *myself* in the process."

Linda is becoming more realistic. She is beginning to see that *she* isn't her work. Linda is God's child. She belongs to Him. She is of infinite worth, and He has endowed her with good gifts.

Who am I? A woman who needs to know I belong, I am worthwhile, and I am capable.

Listen Here, Child!

Even the innocence of childhood play, influenced by the power of the media, can help us form unrealistic expectations of ourselves.

I was reminded of this as I watched my young neighbor, Elizabeth, tearing the pink birthday paper off a baby doll. Her five-year-old mouth formed an exaggerated pout. "But I want a Barbie!" Her parents didn't approve of Barbie for a child so young. Elizabeth's mother told me that Barbie sort of gave her the creeps. But Elizabeth played "Barbies" at her friends' houses anyway, and it wasn't long before her mother caved in to the begging. For Christmas Elizabeth got her Barbie with all the trimmings.

With her generous bosom, tiny waist, and small hips, Barbie and her perfect boyfriend Ken represent a way of life for almost every little American girl. Barbie's lifestyle is complex. She is one of the rich and famous. You can tell by her incredible clothes—silver evening gowns, fur coats, and diamond rings. She has swimming pools and cars, fantastic homes, and dream vacation spots. Barbie and her Ken represent the American fantasy and plant the seeds of unrealistic expectation of real life in the lives of many little girls.

Messages Children Hear

Elizabeth heard about Barbie from her friends. And from babyhood on, she watched television with commercials about Barbies and thousands of other items flashing before her eyes and impressing her brain. She often ignored the programs but paid attention to the fast-moving advertisements.

Elizabeth clapped her hands and laughed at the Poppin' Fresh Pillsbury Doughboy. She learned to repeat the commercial jingles. She sang the Campbell's Soup song in her high chair. At two Elizabeth could shop from her spot in the shopping cart. She pointed and grabbed for certain toys, boxes of cereal, candy, soft drinks, and juice. She knew what she should buy!

Today studies tell us that TV influences what and how a child thinks. Recently, I read that the average preschooler watches up to fifty-four hours of television per week.[1] It's no wonder that the constant messages flashing into our living rooms are defining life. Children not only watch "Sesame Street," but they also watch "As the World Turns" and "Dallas."

Children become passive, waiting to be constantly entertained. Unrealistic.

Children watch extravagant commercials of living dolls and roaring tanks believing the toys they beg for will be bigger than life. Unrealistic.

Children see complex life problems of the "beautiful people" being solved in a thirty-minute sitcom or one-hour soap. Unrealistic.

Children view extreme violence through cartoons, movies,

and even on-the-spot, live-action news, and they believe violence is the way to solve problems. Unrealistic.

Many of us were these children.

A child needs time to explore in order to find out who she is and who she is becoming. She needs creative time to imagine. She needs to dress up and pretend. To paint. To play in the mud. To run in the grass. To feel water on her skin and sun on her face. To watch clouds and to wonder. The child within us needs to know she is unique. One of a kind. Created by God.

Who am I? I am a child who needs to examine life herself and then, in freedom, enjoy creation.

Mangled Messages Teenagers Hear

Society bombs women with messages. If we are sucked in (and most of us are to some extent), we learn to worry about our image. Society promotes the perfect image over personal character. We are told to wrap the package right and worry about what's inside later.

Our fragile wrapping gets torn by daily living, and we spend most of our lives trying to rewrap or patch the package. Even though we may manage to portray the "good life" on the outside, it is the content of the package, the depth and richness of our character, that counts. It is growth within that makes us more real. Our everyday culture rarely touches this idea.

Teenage girls are fully aware how they should look and act. TV, movies, magazines, videos, and music let them know everything they need to know. They know that they must conform to be acceptable.

Madison Avenue's "hot talk" pressures them into the right designer clothes, cosmetics, and cars. If they hurt, they know to take Mediprin if they "don't have time for the pain." And if Mediprin doesn't work, they find a pill that will. They know they'll have more fun if they drink Bud Light with Spuds MacKenzie, the party animal.

Their favorite musicians sing about sex, not romance. They know that being a virgin is old hat. To be "in" they must have a meaningful sexual relationship. If they aren't involved sexually, they learn to lie about it to their friends.

Our culture's messages about packaging really show up at America's high school prom. Today's girls spend the day in tanning booths, getting facials and manicures and hairdos before slipping into that one-of-a-kind dress. They slide into stretch limos or rented BMW convertibles to be whisked off to the ballroom. The band plays and off they float into their dream. This is it! And it only cost $1,000 or more.[2]

But what happens when they get home after the prom—when they kick off the heels and unzip the dress? When the trappings come off, who are they? They are the victims of mangled messages coming from all directions. All they wanted to do was fit in—to belong.

Messages Modern Women Hear

The messages we believe about ourselves at seventeen are enlarged upon the rest of our lives—unless something breaks into our thinking. Yuppies continue to buy all the toys and extras that the media tells them successful people must own. The price tags of their pleasures will announce to society that they have made it. They are validated. They are given worth by their package wrappings.

Women on the move are told at dress-for-success symposiums "you are what you wear." So women rush out and buy "natural fibers"—the speaker's idea of what looks right. We must stay young and trim, so the next step is to join health clubs and diet centers so someone can tell us who we should be—on the outside.

We must make sure our breath is sweet, and we have no body odor, no sags, no bags, no wrinkles. Our teeth must be white and our cheeks a healthy pink (brushed on with the newest cosmetics).

Now there is nothing wrong with looking good and staying

healthy. In fact, everything is right with taking care of our bodies—if we don't stop there.

We are more than our bodies. So our culture tells us to develop our minds and understand our emotions. Then we will know who we are.

We are told that modern women need to have sophisticated ideas. We listen to bright sociologists and psychologists at seminars. Their words influence us. Now, they say, abortion is merely a woman making a choice about her body, not killing life. Living together unmarried is accepted as healthy. Living in chastity is neurotic. Being single and celibate is downright sick, not simply a matter of personal preference.

We are flooded with how-to books telling us how to make love, how to eat, and how to raise children. We rush to counselors to discuss how we feel. We take classes on how to communicate, how to get ahead, and how to live, and we come away with stacks of xeroxed copies for reference. With all this flood of information, it is no wonder we can't trust ourselves.

Whom Can We Trust?

Penny works as a nurse at a diet center where she counsels women. I asked her what she thought about the mangled messages we have to fight through. "Let me put it this way," she said. "I think a lot of the information can be helpful, but the problem is that often we don't THINK. We leave the thinking up to the experts."

Penny was quiet for a minute, then she said, "Some people join every parade. Before we follow the crowd, we really need to wrestle with ideas. We need to know our own values."

How important it is to explore who we are—deep inside the package. How important it is for us to THINK, to sort the messages, to decide what comes in and what stays out of us.

And we have the Holy Counselor within us to guide our thinking. If only we will stop listening to the pounding messages from the outside and listen to the still small voice within us. For God, our Lover, the One we can trust, waits there. "Here I am! I stand at the door and knock. If anyone hears My voice and opens the door, I will come in and eat with him, and he with Me" (Rev. 3:20, NIV).

Who am I? A woman who needs to stretch beyond the influences of my home and culture to discover my uniqueness in the sight of God.

The Curse of Perfectionism

My friend and I were happily spraying ourselves with Chanel no. 5 and scooping up tiny samples of expensive eye cream in Robinson's cosmetic department when a woman in dark sunglasses nudged me.

"I've just had plastic surgery. I'm simply thrilled." She whipped off her sunglasses, exposing yellow bruises and puffy eyes. "Once this swelling is gone, I'm going to be a new woman!" I wondered if her longing to be a new woman came because she had unrealistic expectations of herself—the old woman.

Today there is more nipping and tucking, breast lifting, implanting, and nose bobbing than ever before. Liposuctions suck the fat off all the right places. The perfect, forever-young body is in—growing old gracefully is out. Some women are obsessed with having "hard bodies" and work out for hours in gyms six or seven days a week. Many women who never go "under the knife" or hit the gyms wish they could. It is totally unrealistic to think we can hold back the press of age forever. The only alternative is to die young!

Each of our bodies is unique—a gift from our Creator. Genetically we are different in height, weight, color of skin and eyes, physical strength, and endurance. We are responsible to try and keep ourselves healthy but not perfect. How often do we say: "If only I were thinner, taller or shorter, had thick hair, red hair, or blond hair, or if only I looked like Elizabeth, then I would feel better"? This longing for the perfect look often symbolizes our drive for control and perfection within.

According to medical authorities, 1 out of every 250 female adolescents will develop anorexia nervosa, and without treatment 15 out of 100 anorexics will die. Anorexia nervosa may only seem like an obsession to be thin, but the truth is these young women are perfectionists. While they know they can't be entirely perfect, they can be perfectly thin. This mind-set is a potential killer.

Thinking we should be flawless is a devastatingly unrealistic expectation. A real joy stealer! This ideal is promoted through the messages we receive from parents, peers, schools, and church. Trying to be perfect can lead us to:

- *dishonesty* (We have to lie to be "nice" and keep everyone happy.)
- *illusion* (We have to stay in control to be perfect.)
- *denial* (We cannot let ourselves know we have made mistakes.)
- *defensiveness* (We cannot let others show us our mistakes.)

The bottom line is that perfectionists live in fear—fear of being their real, imperfect selves. Our Lord constantly tells us to "fear not." He is not asking us to be perfect but to be in relationship with Him. He wants us to embrace our humanness. He wants us to release our unrealistic expectation of being perfect. Only God is perfect.

The Addiction of Perfection

A woman who strives for perfection becomes addicted to her ideal. Sometimes the sickness of her unrelenting pressure leads her to search for comfort and relief—often in the wrong places.

In her book *When Society Becomes An Addict*, Anne Wilson Schaef writes:

It may be hard to picture addicts as conscientious, concerned people with high aspirations and high expectations of themselves, but that is what most of them are. Alcoholics, drug addicts, compulsive overeaters are perfectionists. They are convinced that nothing they do is ever good enough, that *they* don't do as much as they should, and that *they* can be perfect if only they figure out how.

Those who treat addicts consider perfectionism to be a major stumbling block to recovery. . . . It is difficult to help addicts forgive themselves for not being perfect and perceive themselves as good people anyway. They persist in viewing themselves as *bad* people trying to become good, not sick people trying to get well.[3]

Under the stress of perfectionism and competition, some women crack. Their unrealistic expectations take an extreme toll on their lives. They see no way to health. Joy is a fairy-tale word. They commit suicide.

It is well known that alcoholism, drug addiction, and eating disorders have a death wish associated with the illness. Alarming statistics concerning women and actual suicides press the seriousness of this point. Young girls, teens, young women, middle-age women, and older women from all walks of life choose to give up life because they can no longer cope with the pain. The American Medical Association reports that female physicians are four times more likely to commit suicide than other women because of the pressure of perfectionism.[4]

For suicide victims life seems to be a curse instead of a gift. Many have lived with the ache of unresolved unrealistic expectations of themselves. They have been overcome by the Depression Vulture, and he has led the way to death.

Let us learn to accept our humanness with its rough edges. Embracing our failures as an essential learning tool common to humans, let us be patient with ourselves. Then we can throw off the affliction of perfectionism.

Life is a gift. We can take up our life and live it with Him, knowing *He* will be in control. *He* will be our perfection—if we let Him. Proverbs remind us: "In his heart a man plans his course, but the Lord determines his steps" (Prov. 16:9, NIV). I never have to live my life floundering alone. He and I are in this together. If I give God my life, we will make it into something of beauty.

Who am I? An imperfect woman who needs to embrace my humanity and let God hold my small hand.

The Curse of Comparison

I'm sure God thinks comparisons are odious. After all, He made each one of us to suit His pleasure. Many of us fail to understand this.

Aileen, a forty-year-old artist, shared her insights with me. "When I was young, I suffered from depression—dark days rolled into weeks then months of living hell. I went to a counselor, but it didn't seem to help. A doctor said I had PMS, so I took lots of vitamin B. I still had bouts of depression.

"Then I found myself in a revealing pattern. It seemed like every time I geared myself up to enter a juried art show I got depressed, and of course, I couldn't paint. I thought maybe it was because I didn't want to be in competition with other artists. And I'm sure that was some of it, but I discovered something more." Aileen drew a quick sketch on a small pad and shoved it toward me. A large figure towered above a tiny figure curled up in a ball.

"You see, I felt like *I* was going to be judged." She smiled and leaned back in her chair. "I'm not in that kind of competition anymore. I met the Judge and He loves me."

Aileen discovered that she was God's handiwork. Her life with Him was co-creation and is never finished.

We all compare ourselves with each other. Our role models help us define what it is to be a woman. But woe to us who stop there. When we reach across the boundaries of our own unique being and believe we should re-create ourselves to become like another person, we are in trouble. The "if onlys" take over our thoughts as we try to imitate the person we perceive has it all. Trying to be someone else, we miss our gift of life—being ourselves!

Competition appears in all sorts of areas. Who's the most beautiful? Who's the most athletic? Who's the most intuitive? Who's the most intelligent? Who's the strongest leader? Who's the most faith filled? Who's the most musical? The list is endless. "Who's the most" begins to translate into "She is more than I am."

I always wanted to be intelligent—really intelligent. I made good grades in school. My teachers labeled me an overachiever. I knew that I didn't have the academic brilliance of some of my peers. My lab partner in high school chemistry didn't seem to care a flip about her grades, but she understood chemistry. I, on the other hand, studied like crazy, learned the formulas, and made straight A's. After the final exam, I promptly forgot all the chemistry I knew, but my old chemistry partner now has her master's in chemical engineering.

My SAT scores were average. My research papers won high grades but never set the world on fire. Where could I make my mark? I tried my hand at art but decided that the world could live without my paintings. Of course, I had help in encouraging this self-criticism. Everywhere I turned I met critics. I didn't understand that their comments were basically meant to help me. My shaky self-image was being worn down to the nub.

Gradually, I am learning to shake off my negativism and, with my Maker, celebrate myself. I have begun to realize that He created me exactly as He desired, IQ and all.

Discovering Our Gifts

A few years ago my friend Rebecca, who teaches high school humanities, burst into my kitchen waving a *U.S. News and*

World Report. She pointed to an article by Howard Gardner, a Harvard University psychologist. "Just wait until you read this. I'm running off copies for all my kids!" I poured over the article with enthusiasm.

> Intelligence is not an absolute such as height that can be measured simply, largely because people have multiple intelligences rather than one single intelligence.
>
> In all, I have identified seven forms of intelligence. The two that are valued most highly in this society are linguistic and logical-mathematical intelligences. When people think of someone as smart, they are usually referring to those two, because individuals who possess linguistic and logical-mathematical do well on tests that supposedly measure intelligence.
>
> But there are five kinds of intelligence that are every bit as important: Spatial, musical, bodily-kinesthetic and two forms of personal intelligence—interpersonal, knowing how to deal with others and intrapersonal, knowledge of self. None of these ought to have priority over others.[5]

Hooray! It was refreshing to read Gardner's research and confirm what I had been learning through the years. My gifts are varied and their worth can't be measured. My job isn't to covet someone else's intellectual gifts but to discover my own.

Who am I? I am a woman who can explore and rejoice in the use of my "intelligences."

Cherishing Our Differences

What a paradoxical life we live. We desperately want to be individuals, and yet the impressions from the media and other facets of our society are so powerful that our culture begins to define us. We are pressured to fit in—look alike, think alike, act alike. Mass media and peer pressure dictate who we are supposed to be. We fail to understand that discovering who we are is life's primary adventure. We need to focus on exploring ourselves, accepting our limitations, and enjoying, disciplining, and giving away our gifts. We need to tell our own unique story. It is time we cherished our differences.

The preschool I directed was staffed by seventeen women. The teachers were teamed in pairs. Before summer vacation I assigned the teacher-teams for the fall session. I tried to put women together whose different strengths would complement each other.

One morning before school Barbara came into my office and shut the door. "I just want you to know that I CAN'T teach with Marcy next year so don't team us!"

"Why not?" I asked. I was making my final decisions and really wanted her input.

"We don't think alike about anything. We're about as different as day and night. It would be a disaster if we shared a room!" I understood her point. We feel more comfortable when we work and socialize with people who are like us. We have a sense of belonging. But can we belong and also be different?

I decided to offer a workshop for my staff on personality differences. After giving us the Myers-Briggs Type Indicator to measure our personality patterns, our workshop leader explained what our patterns meant. Obviously we had God-given differences, and accepting these differences in ourselves and each other could help us work together even better.

We recognized that our "type" was not the definition of ourselves but our "address." It gave us a starting point of understanding. This helped us appreciate each other's strengths and tolerate each other's weaknesses as we worked together throughout the year.

I did not team Barbara and Marcy together that fall, but the following year Barbara requested a room with Marcy. Her reason? "Marcy looks at things differently than I do," said Barbara. "I could use her strengths."

We are robbed of the joy of our own potential when we envy and criticize another's gifts. "If only" I could teach like he does. "If only" I could sing like she does. "If only" I had her wisdom.

One day I realized that if each Christian is a part of my body as Paul teaches, then each Christian's gift actually belongs to me. And my gift belongs to each of them. All of us together make up the same body. How then can I be envious of myself? I am called to co-create with God in order to discover and develop fully what unique gifts and personality I have—and help others do the same. Now I see that their gifts make me more complete. Their strengths make me stronger.

Who am I? A woman with God-given gifts who can discover, develop, and share them with others.

Our Spiritual Search

Jennifer invited me to her house for spinach quiche and fruit salad to meet her neighbor. "Belinda's fascinating," Jennifer told me. "You'll love her."

I *was* fascinated. Putting both hands around my mug of coffee, I let the heat penetrate my palms as Belinda talked. One word followed another. They all sounded deep and mysterious. So powerful. But I was uneasy.

"I study the words of Swami Muktananda. Do you know of him?"

I shook my head.

"He says we should worship and honor ourselves because God dwells in us *as us*. Since I've been using my mantra and meditating, I have really tapped into my own resources." I looked up at Belinda's doe-brown eyes. She did seem peaceful. "Barbra, meditation would really help you know yourself."

We are spiritual, physical, emotional beings. It is no wonder searching for spiritual power has historically been a preoccupation of humankind. Today is no different. The New Age movement is a mixture of pop psychology, Hindu beliefs, and spirit worship. Its tentacles wrap themselves throughout our culture, explaining to us that everyone and everything is part of God and part of a divine oneness within.

In his book *Unmasking the New Age*, Douglas Groothuis defines the New Age movement as monism, the belief that all that exists is one. There is then no real difference between God, a person, or a mountain. "There are not many selves but one Self, the One."[6]

New Agers say our search for who we are spiritually is over. We simply look within ourselves for all the answers. With, of course, the help of psychic sojourners—channelers, spiritualists, palm readers, mind readers, witches, and gurus—we are encouraged to be transformed by our own potential. They tell us the ultimate good lies dormant within us. With their guidance through the supernatural, they say each of us can let the good and the beautiful emerge.

Belinda and I are worlds apart in our faith. Believing that everyone and everything is part of God is monism. I believe that God is separate from His creation. He is the Maker. I am the made. He alone, not myself or any part of His creation, is worthy to be worshiped. As I turn myself over to God and grow in His image, He will empower me with the Holy Spirit. Belinda turns to herself for spiritual answers. I turn to God.

Who am I? I am a woman who loves and worships her Creator, and who is empowered by Him.

I Am God's Child

The iced tea glass stood empty in a ring of water. The magazines lay scattered on the rug. My mind and heart stood together in reflection from my afternoon of solitude. "Who am I supposed to be?"

I know so much of who I am not. I am not beautiful. I am

not young. I am not brilliant. I am not athletic. I am not perfect. But I *am!* God in His great mystery has decided He wants ME. So by an act of His will He brought me into creation. Unique. One of a kind. He imprinted me with all the marks of that uniqueness so I would never forget. My handprints and footprints, the curl and folds of my ears, and even my blood hold the special secrets of myself and no one else.

God had no reason for making me other than that He delights in my fellowship. He does not need me. He needs nothing. After all, He is God. But He wants me.

Who am I? I am a child of the Living God. I am a living temple, and He has breathed His Spirit into my small house and filled me with gifts. Some of the gifts I am exploring. Some I have unwrapped, tossed aside, and need to rediscover. Some gifts wait to be opened.

Who am I? I am God's child who is still becoming. He is not demanding perfection. He is encouraging risk and growth. He is not demanding that I be "nice." He wants me to live in truth. He is not demanding I stay young. He wants me to live in reality. He is not demanding that I be sophisticated. He wants me to live simply with Him.

He asks me to let go of unrealistic expectations of my world and myself—these unrealistic expectations that steal my joy—the joy of being me. If I let go of what *they* say, maybe I can listen to more of what He is saying.

I stretched my legs and stood up. I walked through the house to the kitchen and filled my empty glass with cold water. It reminded me of His words: "Whoever drinks of the water that I shall give him shall never thirst" (John 4:14).

I had been with Him. And I knew who I was. I was no longer thirsty.

Thinking It Through

1. How has our culture influenced who you are?
2. List some of *your* own values. Where do you get your

value system? From others? From yourself?
3. Do you love and value yourself as much as you value others? In what specific ways do you show love to yourself?
4. Have you ever wished you were someone else? Who and why?
5. In what ways are you a perfectionist?
6. List the ways in which you are unique.
7. How would you describe your temperament?
8. What are your areas of intelligence?
9. What are your special God-given gifts?
10. What gifts might you explore and discipline in the future?
11. How do you care for your body? Your mind? Your spirit?
12. How do you know you are God's beloved child?
13. How do you love and appreciate yourself?
14. Can you celebrate yourself? How?
15. List the ways in which you belong, you are worthwhile, and you are capable.

"See how great a love the Father has bestowed upon us, that we should be called children of God; and such we are"
(1 John 3:1).

Chapter Five

WHOM CAN I BELIEVE?
Unrealistic Expectations of Authorities

T he long twilight held on to the last shadows of the day as I sat with friends after the Fourth of July picnic. Fireworks are not allowed anymore, but the children next door drew light designs in the sky with sparklers. Sweet juice and black seeds filled my mouth from my last bite of watermelon. Somewhere in the distance I heard "The Star-Spangled Banner." Folding my legs underneath me, I sank back against the chaise lounge, content with my day, myself, and my country.

"America is wonderful," I said.

"Best country in the world," said Sheri. "Wouldn't want to live anywhere else. But we've got some big problems." I didn't want to think about problems and disrupt the peace, so I tried to change the subject.

The last of the sun slipped away and the dark dropped over us like a blanket. "Can you believe this beautiful night?" I looked up at the stars. "Just think. We're seeing light that's been traveling for thousands of years."

"You know, one thing that worries me is government spending," said Sheri. "If I ran my finances like the government runs theirs, I'd have to file for bankruptcy! The U.S. debt's going to run us as deep as the heavens."

"For Pete's sake, don't talk about all that now," said Liz. "You'll ruin the night. Besides, you know Congress will just raise taxes or declare a war to balance the budget." She laughed.

As the conversation rambled on, I began to listen to my own inner thinking. I didn't want to bother about the complex problems of our government. Besides, what could I do about it? Wasn't it *their* job to keep the country steady? I read the *L.A. Times* and *Newsweek*. I watch the NBC national news at 7 P.M. I vote. It was up to *them* to do the rest. Well, wasn't it?

Government: Won't You Support Me?

Americans' attitude toward the United States government contains a mixture of faith and suspicion. But in the end we let the government think for us.

We believe that the President and Congress will meet with kings and queens, ambassadors, dictators, and presidents of other countries and solve world problems. They will fund our mighty military forces to protect our peace. They will manipulate our dollar to avoid another depression. They will provide solutions to the internal labor problems and the international trade balance. They will attack crime. Stop drugs. Save the elderly and the poor. Address health care. End poverty. Protect justice.

Most of us draw our conclusions about the issues from the overload of information that comes to us in a barrage of words from TV newscasters and newspaper journalists. Even if we are political science majors or financial or military wizards, our conclusions may be only half thought-out—partly because we are only receiving half-truths.

At work or social gatherings we may defend our viewpoint with energy; however, if we seriously examine how much we actually know about the subject, we would probably back off.

Muddled from conflicting stories, most of us throw up our

hands. We'll let *them* handle it. One way or another the government will probably take care of us. After all, we pay taxes.

This skeptical but relaxed attitude keeps us blind concerning the forces of power that exist for themselves and not the good of the people—the organizations that embody evil rather than good. "Institutions can and do often become nothing more than organized sin."[1] Still, we hate to believe this even when we are face-to-face with the evidence.

It is simply not true that all individuals' needs will be cared for by Mother America. The evidence slapped me in the face as I parked my car one hot, smoggy afternoon on Los Angeles' west side near the L.A. County Hospital. As I walked to my meeting, I tried not to look at the small woman slumped against the faded peach building. "Some change. Some change, lady." She shook a battered shoe box with one hand and hugged her brown-sacked bottle with the other. I picked up my pace.

Three dirty, barefoot kids darted between parked cars yelling "chicken," while a bent, white-haired woman waved her arms and shouted at them in Spanish.

A half-naked toddler, her face streaked with dirt, stood crying alone on the sidewalk. I stopped, wondering what I should do. A young black-eyed boy about six or seven appeared and grabbed the baby by the arm and yanked her down the alley.

Wherever I looked, poverty looked back. I was heartsick and shared my feelings with my friend. "It's a shame but don't worry," he said. "They all know how to work the system. They're on welfare. Let the government take care of them. It's not your concern."

All citizens are hopeful that the mysterious, powerful *they* will bring relief to the hungry and homeless through the welfare system—but we are also cynical. We know there are a lot of holes in the almighty system.

Cynthia is a perfect example. At twenty-one Cynthia, her eight-month-old daughter, and her nineteen-month-old son waited alone in a downtown Chicago one room apartment for her young husband, Terry, to bring home some food. Unable to face his hungry family, Terry never came home.

"It got darker and darker. I was terrified," said Cynthia. "There was no formula for the baby—nothing. Finally, I knew Terry wasn't coming home. The kids cried themselves to sleep and woke up crying. My neighbor gave us something to eat and bus money to get to the welfare office.

"I was so scared and so tired when I got there. I filled out the forms, and they said if I was eligible they'd send me a check in two weeks. But I was desperate. I didn't even have money to get back home."

Cynthia fell through the cracks in the system, but fortunately, through a church in downtown Chicago, she found help.

Consider the middle-aged woman who, because she earned money baby-sitting, could not get financial aid for herself and her three children. She had to give up her job to receive welfare.

As a nation, we are committed to helping the poor. But it is unrealistic to think our welfare system can serve all our poor and create perfect solutions to the self-defeating features that benefit checks create.

The welfare system (and the justice system, the educational system, the military system, etc.) needs reform. It will always need reform. And it is unrealistic to think *they* will revamp the systems unless each individual enters with interest at some level. After all, the government isn't really *they*. In a democracy it is *we*.

I believe we should think. Most of us have unrealistic expectations about our government—not only concerning its welfare system, but all the systems it has arranged for us. We must be realistic about the government's power to solve all the international, national, and personal problems of war, famine, finances, racism, justice, and health. As I heard recently, "The government is not our friend; the government is an instrument."

We hope, we pray that our government, under the leadership of our elected officials, will have the power and the wisdom to take care of us. We trust that our great military will protect us from enemy assault. And when we are old, we look forward to leaning back into the arms of Social Security and Medicare, believing that we are owed a debt. We must be realistic here too. Is it possible for the government to have enough money accrued when the surge of baby boomers hits the system at retirement age?

And what about the justice system? Right now the judges who interpret the Constitution seem to be stripping away the Judeo-Christian moral principles on which our country was founded. Our justice system is based on the interpretation of the law, not necessarily on what is just. Often we hear of big-time Mafia or white-collar embezzlers being set free or serving a short prison sentence while small-time criminals are locked up for years.

The systems are entrapped in systems of their own, bound by laws spoken and unspoken. The systems within the systems often exist to serve themselves—not to serve others.

We must not expect these systems to save us. We must throw off the belief that if we simply accept and conform to the system, we can have everything we need and everything we want. Let us embrace God, not the systems, as the One we can trust.

Individual contributions. So how do we make a difference?

• By searching for our own personal outreach, individually we can make a difference.

• By taking responsibility for our own lives, we can look at Uncle Sam and the promise of a "chicken in every pot" more realistically.

• By being informed and honest both individually and as a nation, we can admit our errors and our evils, and we can work for truth and justice.

• By working at whatever level we can to make the systems more accountable, we can demand that the systems serve the citizens instead of themselves.

• By praying that our leaders would have wisdom and would return to the faith, we can serve our nation and our God.

There are many quiet heroes in our country—heroes making a difference. For example, my Grandmother Goodyear told me about her own personal welfare system.

"We didn't have any money on the farm during the Depression, but God blessed us with food. When anybody came up to the house hungry, I fed him and Grandpa put him to work. If he was a serious worker we'd keep him on until he got his footing."

In my own community Valerie Scott knew firsthand what it was like to be hungry and homeless. When she was blessed with better days, she began cooking, canning, and drying food in her own kitchen to serve the hungry. Her ministry grew so large she needed help, so Operation Outreach was born as a nondenominational Christian community project. Those in need and those who can work pull together in community gardens, food distribution, counseling, job placement, and ministry. They are realistic about their present needs. The project works because each person brings his God-given gift to share.

Ken Wheeler grew up in a Los Angeles housing project. He saw the horror of gang killings. One of those killings took the life of Ken's best friend. Now Ken risks his own life counseling gang members on the night streets of L.A.

Newsweek wrote a story about Therese Rocco who took over the missing persons police unit twenty-seven years ago in Pittsburgh. She dedicated herself to work past the constraints of the system. She stays involved because of her compassion and commitment and now helps track an average 120 lost persons a month, most of them runaway children.[2]

We can be realistic about ourselves. Not many of us will run for President or start an orphanage, but each of us has a gift to give. Large or small, each gift makes a definite difference. Ask God to help you explore your gift, open up your ministry, and help you become a giver in your community, a giver in our country, and a giver in our world. We listen to David when he says, "Trust in the Lord, and do good; dwell in the land and cultivate faithfulness" (Ps. 37:3).

Medical System: Won't You Save Me?

America has one of the finest medical and mental health care systems in the world, but good health care is expensive. We expect our country will take care of our suffering. The truth is that many of our citizens are turned away from clinics and hospitals while empty hospital beds wait for properly insured patients.

Patricia Brenner, R.N., Ph.D., says:

Health care has become a commodity. . . . During the last fifteen years the health-care environment has switched from non-profit to profit based, from community-based organizations with volunteerism and planned charity to corporate-based ownership with accidental charity. . . . The business contract view of the health-care provider patient relationship turns the patient into a customer to be sold a bill of goods. The convenantal relationship between health-care providers and patients is lost altogether.[3]

Many Americans cannot buy their way into the health care market nor do they fit the description of those eligible to receive free health care. They go without medical attention.

Those of us who do make it into the system often hold unrealistic expectations about the healers. We give them charge over our bodies and the bodies of our loved ones, expecting them to make us well. We take our broken bodies and broken hearts to doctors and counselors, hoping they will "fix" us and send us on our way. If we are not helped, some of us go from specialist to specialist. Others of us grow cynical and retreat into our pain.

Doctor as Powerful Healer. In our society doctors represent power. While we sit in revealing paper gowns, they stand over us silently feeling and listening to our bodies. We dress and squirm in our seats as the doctor sits behind the desk. What is he thinking? What will he say? What will he make us do? More tests? Medication? The hospital? The doctor seems to hold the words of our life or death.

Today's doctors must assimilate a tremendous amount of technical information. The health care field is filled with some of our country's most brilliant women and men. It's no wonder we hold them in highest esteem. Our quality of life depends on our mental and physical health, so why wouldn't we be awed and impressed by our mental and physical healers?

Somehow we have come to believe that M.D. means "Medical Deity." We take ourselves to the doctors and expect them to heal our bodies. We take ourselves to counselors and expect them to heal our minds. What we often fail to realize is that God is the healer. The professionals are His assistants, and we must be realistic about their roles.

Take Sally, for example. Dr. Clark looked at the X rays and listened carefully to Sally's chest. "Sally, you have pneumonia. I want you to have strict bed rest." Dr. Clark ripped the prescriptions off her pad and handed them to Sally. "I'll see you in one week."

The doctor goes on to her next patient. Sally feels relieved. Maybe she should have told Dr. Clark about the pain in her stomach, but she didn't want to be a complainer. Anyway she's got a diagnosis and medication. Of course she can't take off work for a whole week—maybe a few days.

Sally shuffles out of the office, picks up her prescriptions, and goes to bed. She feels somewhat better in three days and drags back to work. Well, what else can she do? She can't use all her sick days up, can she?

After a week Sally is back in the office for a recheck— listless, coughing, feverish, and angry. "Whatever you gave me sure didn't help, Dr. Clark!" Sally's unrealistic expectations are obvious.

Why do we give medical authorities so much power over our lives? In my case, I learned as a child not to question the doctor. At four years old I had rheumatic fever. Laying flat in bed for the next six months, I learned in no uncertain terms to do exactly as Dr. Katie told me. If I didn't cry when I got the blood tests, if I didn't ask questions, I was a good girl. And I wanted to be a good girl.

At twenty years old I was diagnosed as having systemic lupus. With swollen joints, mouth full of lesions, high fever, and kidney problems, I was transferred from a small hospital in Cheyenne, Wyoming to a large teaching hospital in Denver, Colorado. Dr. Mays was in charge of my case.

It never occurred to me, as I submitted to test after test, that I should ask why, what, who, and how, much less dare to say no to anything. Dr. Mays was the Medical Deity. I was only the patient. I waited every day with the Depression Vulture perched on the end of my bed for his visit. Finally, coming through the door, followed by a stream of young white-coated interns, Dr. Mays would explain my case, ask a few questions, read my chart, and leave.

I did all he said. I was waiting for him to make me well. Unapproachable Dr. Mays was godlike to me. I gave him full power over my life as I'd been taught to do when I was a child. If I didn't get well, it was his fault not mine.

Fortunately for me, Dr. Mays was a good physician, but through the years I have had to learn to accept responsibility for my own body and use my physicians as medical counselors. I have had to learn to see myself as body, mind, emotions, and spirit—all of which deeply affect one another in sickness and in health.

Doctor As Servant. In his book *The Healing of Persons*, Dr. Paul Tournier writes to his fellow physicians urging them to realize that God alone is the great Healer, and they are to be God's instruments of this healing. Tournier encourages men and women of medicine to work toward a broader role than that of a powerful, aloof professional. He says that besides being a scientist, a doctor must be a servant to his patients and help them with their deeper problems. Tournier asks:

> But how are we to help our patients resolve their personal problems? How are we to develop our personal influence over them? Science and technique can be taught. Moral authority, however, comes not by scientific training but from our own spiritual maturity, and from the experience of our own lives, from the answers we have found to our own personal problems through the grace of God.[4]

Dr. Bernie Siegel, in his book *Love, Medicine, and Miracles*, reports that being a health professional often takes great personal toll. Doctors have more problems with drugs and alcohol and have a higher suicide rate than their patients. They feel more hopeless than their patients and die faster after the age of sixty-five.

Dr. Siegel says, "No wonder many people are reluctant to go to mainstream physicians. Would you go to a mechanic who couldn't get his own car to run?"[5]

We must remember that counselors, nurses, doctors, and psychiatrists are not magicians. They are people in process with problems of their own. Some have learned, and others are beginning to learn the art of healing. Others, although they have scientific knowledge, may not understand what it takes to involve the patient in her own recovery—to love herself enough to get well. We have to be realistic. We cannot view medical professionals as gods.

My doctor of thirteen years has become my partner in health and a spiritual friend. Dr. Robert Gerber is a brilliant man with natural compassion for his patients, but after having a spiritual experience with the Lord, Dr. Gerber has become a true partner in healing. He gives medical and spiritual leadership to his patients. He hugs the weak, touches the old, and listens to the cries of a heavy heart. He prays for us all and asks for our prayers. He also asks that we fully participate, taking responsibility for our lives.

God is my Maker. Dr. Gerber is my coach. Together we aim the gun and shoot the Depression Vulture out of the sky.

How Can We Get Well? We need to let go of unrealistic expectations of the medical system. How can we do this?

● We can take responsibility for our own lives. We can think and act on our own behalf.

● We can use our doctors as resources and plan our course of action with them.

● We can understand that the health of our emotions, mind, and spirit deeply influences the health of our body.

● We can get proper nutrition and exercise.

● We can play and laugh.

● We can learn to love ourselves enough to get well.

● We can understand that suffering is a part of living. It is through suffering that we are forced to change, to grow, and to seek God.

Margaret has bone cancer. The challenge of her illness has made a profound change in her life. Margaret no longer looks to her doctor for a cure. She works with his advice to make her life good. She has learned to live life beautifully one moment at a time—with God. Her life has come down to the purest art form of living with Him in love. She told me that in many profound ways she has been deeply healed.

Like Margaret, when medical efforts fail our body (and that time will come), we cling to the promise that in the next life God will wipe the tears from our eyes and resurrect us in new bodies. He is our perfect healer. We can put our expectations in Him and not be disappointed.

Education: Won't You Elevate Me?

From the beginning of time man has wanted to KNOW. Knowledge gives us a sense of power. Take Adam and Eve, for example. God gave them a perfect environment and a perfect relationship with each other and with Himself. He included Adam in a co-creative effort. He had Adam name all the animals. Now in my mind that means Adam had an excellent intellect! But he and Eve were tempted to elevate themselves by eating fruit of the tree of knowledge of good and evil. They could be like God, the serpent said. So they took a bite of knowledge.

Most of us have unrealistic expectations of the educational system. Our culture admires the intellectuals of its time, and we look with awe at the finest universities. Who isn't impressed with a Ph.D. from Harvard, Oxford, or Stanford? We believe a proper education is a step toward safety. By getting a degree (preferably from the best institution possible), we can break down cultural, financial, and racial barriers. We can have professions of worth. We can have better medical benefits. We can make big money. We can have it all!

Educational institutions have the authority to bestow the magic degree that, we believe, has the power to give us happiness and security for the rest of our lives.

Baby Education. We believe in the power of education so firmly that many Americans begin working on their child's education at birth. In some areas, prestigious preschools are in such high demand that babies are put on waiting lists before they are born.

A recent *Cathy* comic strip pokes fun at the state-of-the-art baby education. The four frames of the comic strip all show baby Zenith's toys. In the first frame we see Zenith's animated, interactive, microchip-driven bear with voice, eye, mouth, and paw movements. Next, we see Zenith's hand-crafted Italian teak building block set and her special front suspension tricycle. The third frame shows Zenith's tyrannosaurus puppet that sings the French alphabet and her $300 library of pop-up books from the Museum of Modern Art. Finally, in the last frame we see Zenith's favorite toy: an empty toilet paper tube.[6]

Have children really changed?

A record-breaking 2.5 million three- and four-year-olds are already in classrooms preparing for kindergarten. The pressure to perform academically is growing more intense. Parents want to know why Johnny can't read at age four or five.

When I was a preschool director, I was cornered by an anxious father one parent's night. "I'm not sending my Janet to this preschool to play with blocks. She needs to learn to write the alphabet and print her name. I don't want her to be a kindergarten dropout!"

Explaining that her appropriate work *was* her play, I said she was learning a great deal. Unimpressed by my comments he said, "Don't you realize the importance of these years? We want her to make it into a good college, and she's got to build her basics now."

Play was building the basics. But instead of confident play, Janet nervously worried about getting the "right" answers in circle time. Her self-esteem came through praise from adults for what she knew, so she tried to impress them with information and the words she could read. She was under pressure to perform all the time. I knew it would be difficult for Janet to believe that her Father God loved *her* with no strings attached.

Power of the Teacher. All of us want the benefit of education for ourselves and our children. We know the advantage of a degree in our culture. We hope this advantage will safeguard us from the tragedies of life. A golden education seems to hold the key to happiness and success. But our parents and teachers hold the keys to our education and our self-image.

I pulled the dusty, maroon Friends University Annual from the bookshelf and turned the pages one by one until I found my father's picture. "Chester Meyer Goodyear: Class President, Basketball Captain, Debate Team Winner, Who's Who in American Schools and Colleges." My mother's picture was on the next row. "Leone Hawkins: Inter-Society President, Class Treasurer, YMCA Cabinet, Who's Who in American Schools and Colleges." As a teenager, I wanted to go to college too, but I wasn't sure I could make it. If I did get in, I could never do as well as my parents.

As I sat on the floor with the book in my lap, the memory

of Mrs. Robertson's voice boomed inside my head. I could almost feel the heat from her heavy body and round, red face leaning over my desk. I saw her tapping my paper with the end of her red pencil. I could feel my hands beginning to sweat and my child-body tremble. "Barbra, you just can't think! Look at this! Any fourth-grader should be able to do this simple division!"

Mrs. Robertson shook my confidence to the core. She was my authority and after a year of her verbal slamming, I no longer believed I was capable. Embarrassed by my lack of information and all my imperfections, I grew afraid to risk answering in class. I would probably be wrong! It took another teacher, Dr. Capleanor, in a college botany class to encourage me to participate. By coaxing me to think, to be creative, and to honor the Creator of all knowledge, he began resurrecting my broken self-esteem.

We are thankful for dedicated teachers like Dr. Capleanor—and Ruby Forsythe, who still runs the one-room Episcopal Church day school where she has taught for fifty years. She knows the children in Pawley's Island will have a better chance at life through education and the knowledge of the God who loves them. Some of those youngsters have gone on to the university, and they have gone with realistic expectations because of Ruby Forsythe's teaching. They have learned to use their education but to put their trust in God.[7]

The University System. Those of us outside the inner workings of the university idealistically think of the campus as holding the gleaming towers of thought where the power of thinking is protected and cherished.

The truth is the system is full of politics—men and women striving to "get published," reach tenure, win endowments for their department; professors jockeying for power, seeking independent research projects, leaving the teaching to graduate students. The system is not always helpful to students. Take Sonia, for instance.

Sonia was thirty-nine when she entered a doctoral program

in music, her lifelong dream. It took her five years to complete her studies, and the sixth and seventh years she wrote the full-length symphony which completed her dissertation. Before the music was accepted, Sonia's major professor died. She was assigned a new professor who, after looking over her work, would not accept her music. Sonia was devastated. The seven years allowed for her doctorate were up. Her committee would not go against the major professor's decision. Her Mus.D. was denied. Sonia had a nervous breakdown.

Twelve years have gone by and Sonia has recovered her life. "I had all my dreams linked to my doctorate. I was devastated when my degree was out of reach. I thought my life was over. But through my healing, God lifted me to life, and I have learned to trust in Him instead of a system. I didn't lose my gift." Sonia held up a sheet of intricate black notes. "My music is better than ever!"

College life presented a wealth of learning and stretching for me and most of my friends. However, for some it became a nightmare. Nancy worked harder at her studies than anyone in the dorm. The first in her family to go to college, Nancy felt strongly about doing well. She wanted to excel—for them. During the first semester, she grew so anxious she couldn't sleep the night before a test. Eyes rimmed in black and losing weight, Nancy began taking pills to sleep and pills to wake up.

One night right before Christmas break, I heard her crying in her room. When she wouldn't answer my knock, I pushed open the door. She was curled in a fetal position on her bed; she had taken a whole bottle of sleeping pills. For Nancy, college wasn't security and freedom. During her slow recovery she developed a sense of self-worth—with or without a college degree.

We all know people with degrees who are out of work, unhappily married, angry, broken, and lost. We must be realistic about education. Education is an excellent tool. It can challenge our minds, demand our excellence, and enlarge our vistas. But education is not our salvation. It will not fill every hole. It may elevate us in our culture, but it does not elevate us in God's eyes.

God and Knowledge. The Pharisees were the most learned people of the Jewish sect at the time of Christ. Constantly studying and debating the law, the Pharisees sat under the teachings of great rabbis. They were held in highest respect for their knowledge and were proud of their status. But Jesus said they were blind to the truth.

We puff up and feel safe because of our degrees, but "The LORD knows the thoughts of man, that they are a mere breath" (Ps. 94:11). As honorable as learning is, our collection of knowledge is not as valuable as wisdom from God. He reminds us: "For as the heavens are higher than the earth, so are My ways higher than your ways, and My thoughts than your thoughts" (Isa. 55:9). We must come to worship Him who is Truth.

I do hope all my children go to college. A firm believer in education, I hope they and I will continue to discipline our minds, ask questions, and challenge ourselves to learn new skills and mentally grow.

Those of us who teach and those of us who learn are in a power relationship. We use that system of power to create good. We must remember that education can enrich our lives and offer great cultural benefits—but it will never have the authority to fill and save us. Only God can do that.

Religion: Won't You Fill Me?

"I can pinpoint the beginning of my personal agony over the church the summer I came home in so much pain." Anne's eyes grew red as she shared her story. "I still remember the morning light pouring through the blues, greens, and reds of the stained glass window of Jesus holding a lamb.

"I choked back the lump in my throat and sank against the cushions of the church pew. I didn't want to cry. Not in church. I looked back at the piercing light of the window and then squeezed my eyes shut. I wanted to be that lamb.

"I remember Mrs. Bloomfield rattling on and on—patting me on the shoulder. Mrs. Peters was grinning and waving her white-gloved hand from two pews away. She was such a gossip. I ducked my head.

"The ceremony began. Two ministers, robed in black, walked behind the choir, robed in gold. 'Glory to God in the Highest, Peace on Earth, Good Will Toward Men.' Announcements, hymn, choir, prayer, offering, sermon, hymn. I wanted to cry."

Anne looked in my face, straining to see if I understood. Sighing, she went on.

"It was over. I stood up. My heart pounding. I hurried up the aisle. Oh, I needed God so much. The minister stopped me at the door of the church. 'Glad to see you! I hope you'll be here next Sunday.' His sweaty hand dropped mine as his eyes focused on the man behind me.

"While the people nodded and smiled and chatted on the way out, I slipped through the crowd. They seemed so perfect. I left the air-conditioned sanctuary and was blasted by the summer heat as I hurried down the wide steps of the church.

"When I got into my car, I dropped my head on the steering wheel and sobbed. I had wanted the rigid walls of the church to fall down and the body of Christ to gather me up. I needed healing. I needed comfort. I needed Jesus. Instead I got ritual. I felt afraid. How could I raise my hand and ask for prayer? How could I say my husband had left me, and I was brokenhearted?

"The church wasn't safe." Anne's eyes narrowed. Her words punched with bitterness. "I left that day vowing never to enter the church again."

Religion versus Faith. Like Anne we all have expectations of "the church"—and at some time most of us are let down. We have a deep empty hole which we hope the church will fill; however, we discover that the church is not nurturing enough, not sensitive enough, not loving enough to meet all our needs. And until Christ returns, the church will remain imperfect.

Many of us want the church to tell us what to think, how to worship, and how to live. We want a relationship with the church instead of with God. We want Old Testament religious life. If we follow the church laws, do what the church says, then surely we will be OK with the Almighty.

We don't have to think for ourselves. *We* don't have to be faithful ourselves. *We* don't have to listen to God ourselves. The church will be responsible for our religion. If our religion fails us, we can blame, not ourselves, but the church for our collapse of faith.

As an organization the church is tempted, as is any organization, in areas of politics, money, and power. Meetings go on without any reference to God's purpose. Decisions are made without prayerful consideration. Why? Because much of the church's business is considered just that—business. We forget we are dealing with Holy Business.

We look for super-ministers who can evangelize, teach, preach, counsel, raise funds, keep peace, lead missions, touch the children, and visit the sick. We become addicted to their dynamic personalities, following them wherever they lead. They are the main attraction of the church, and we are the audience. Sometimes these preacher-wonders are almost worshiped. After all, it is so much easier to follow a person we can see than a God we can't see. As grateful as we are for the gifts of these individuals, somewhere along the line our idols will fail. We will collapse when their stardom begins to tarnish, and we discover they are human beings.

What about the people who go to church? The so-called "Christians." They seem peaceful and friendly and holy until some hot issue erupts over buildings vs. missions. Or until the news leaks out that Mr. and Mrs. Jones are filing for divorce. Then the gossip whirls. The Depression Vulture perches on the pulpit and feasts on the results. We could go away so disillusioned with religion, the church, ministers, and "Christians" that we slam the door on faith.

Who's Responsible for My Faith? Jesus was a radical. He made a whip and in a rage drove the money changers from the temple. "Is it not written, 'MY HOUSE SHALL BE CALLED A HOUSE OF PRAYER FOR ALL THE NATIONS'? But you have made it a ROBBERS' DEN" (Mark 11:17). Christ ripped away at the religious system and the pomp of the priests' position. Challenging the elaborate Law, He replaced it with the spirit of faith in Himself—and nothing else.

We can fall into the same trap as the Pharisees, thinking that by following organized church traditions or strong leaders, we automatically have faith. This can never be. It is unrealistic to expect that a church, a pastor, or a group of people can give us God. The organization can give us a religious framework, but faith is personal. Faith is a verb. Faith is an action of the heart. Each of us is responsible to walk our own journey with Christ.

Who Is the Church? We are the church. We are the body of Christ. In order for this body to function, each of us has been given various gifts of the Spirit. That means we cannot expect anyone to be a "star." In a real sense each of us is a "star." The Holy Spirit displays God's power through each of us as a means of helping the entire church.

Paul explains it this way:

> There are different kinds of spiritual gifts, but the same Spirit gives them. There are different ways of serving, but the same Lord is served. There are different abilities to perform service, but the same God gives ability to everyone for their particular service. The Spirit's presence is shown in some way in each person for the good of all" (1 Cor. 12:4-7, GNB).

We are given gifts to give each other—and we are called to love.

I have my days of uneasiness about the church. I feel uneasy about the impersonal, enormous institution. The powerful infighting, the materialism, the politics. I feel suffocated by the pollution and I want to run. I feel like the Christian writer and woman of great faith, Madeleine L'Engle, who said of the church, "It's awful, but it's all we have."[8]

For years I battled in my mind over the church. I wondered if I should belong to an organization I had so much trouble embracing. One morning in despair I prayed, "Lord, the church is a thorn in my side, but she belongs to You. Please—let me see something new in all this."

God began turning my focus. I started realizing *I* was the church. *I* was the church—along with other true believers. My part was to go and give the gifts given to me. My part was to go in love. My part was to help the koinonia fellowship, the fellowship of the Spirit, grow. From that morning on, God began changing my expectation from getting to giving. When I moved into the body with my gifts, I experienced an exchange of gifts, and I came away from the church fed in surprising ways.

Do We Need the Church? Anne held on to her bitterness toward the church for many years. Eventually she came home. "I was so angry that the church had let me down when I needed comfort! One night a friend asked if I'd like to go to her Bible study. It was in this small group of loving people that I began my way back.

"As I healed, I began to realize I wanted the church to do for me what I had to do for myself. I wanted the church to give me a quick-fix for my deep pain. In the end God and I had to deal with my bitterness and hurt. He surrounded me with loving believers for support and counsel—but I had to submit to the work of faith in His love for me."

We need the body of the church because, as Richard Foster points out in his book, *Celebration of Discipline*, we need to exercise the disciplines of confession, worship, guidance, and celebration together. We need to love each other. We are called to be one as the Son and the Father are one. The church is the vehicle for that oneness.

Let us come together. We must work at righting the

wrongs of the church. Then, putting away false expectations of having a perfect church to solve all our dilemmas, let us serve each other in Spirit and in Truth. And in this Spirit and in this Truth, we will experience Love. The true church. The body of Christ.

Whom Can I Believe?

Whom can I believe? Our government, our medical system, our educational system, and our religious system are powerful authorities. We hold unrealistic expectations about these complex systems and give them great power over our lives. We must learn to think. We must learn to be involved at an individual level. We must learn to use these systems as the instruments they were intended to be, working to improve them whenever we can.

Some of us will be called to be servant leaders working within the systems to stamp our values in the schools, the government, the hospitals, and the church. We must learn to carry the power with care—and for the care of others.⁹

Let us remember that God alone is our ultimate authority. He is our Majestic King. He is our Wise Teacher. He is our Mighty Healer. He is the Head of the church.

He alone will fill all the promises of eternal care that He has made and bring us His joy.

Thinking It Through

1. What expectations do you have concerning the welfare system, Social Security, Medicare? Are you realistic?
2. Where do your opinions about the government come from? Are they based on facts or feelings?
3. Do you believe you can personally make a difference? What can you do?
4. How do you view the medical system? How can you cooperate with your doctor and take responsibility for your healing?

5. What are your expectations of the educational system? In what ways are you responsible for your own learning? Do you view education as a tool or as a savior?
6. Are you disappointed in the church? How has the church let you down? How do you identify yourself as a part of the body of Christ, the true church?
7. What are your spiritual gifts? Explain. How do you share them with your church?
8. Are you overly dependent on a powerful minister? Explain.
9. Explain the difference between religion and faith.
10. Are you taking responsibility for your own spiritual growth or depending entirely on your church to feed you? In what ways can you take more responsibility for your own growth?

"I will lift up my eyes to the mountains; from whence shall my help come? My help comes from the LORD who made heaven and earth"

(Ps. 121:1-2).

Chapter Six

WHERE'S MY PRINCE?
Unrealistic Expectations of Husbands and Marriage

I rushed into the Mustard Seed for lunch ten minutes late. Looking around the front dining room, I saw Gail in a corner booth. She looked pensive, her head propped on her hand, peering out the window.

"Gail, sorry I'm late. I—"

"Doesn't matter. Gave me time to think." Gail's gray-green eyes glistened. Even before I sat down her words gushed out. "I wanted you to hear this from me. Donald and I are getting a divorce." Stunned, I sank in my seat. Gail looked into her coffee cup and watched the black swirl she stirred around with her spoon. "My life is slipping by and Donald just isn't there for me."

I had known Gail for eight years. We had shared our trials, our hopes, and our dreams. One of Gail's dreams was that her husband would turn into the prince of her imagination. The Depression Vulture nested in her house, stuffing himself from her pantry full of unrealistic expectations about marriage, robbing her joy.

Over the years Gail had tried everything to make her marriage good. She read the latest marriage tips in *Reader's Digest* and *McCalls*. She talked to friends, listened to tapes. She even tried counseling. Gail wanted Donald to be the romantic lover of her dreams, but nothing she did changed him. Her emptiness seemed to be a bottomless pit of aloneness.

Things started out differently. When Gail and Donald met, they seemed made for each other. From their first encounter, electricity raced between them. Romance filled their days and nights. They were inseparable. Gail told me Donald brought her flowers, phoned her in the middle of the night, and wrote her love letters. In a short time they were married—with stars in their eyes.

"I dreamed of someone who would accept and understand me," said Gail. "Someone who would be intimate and give me the security I needed. I found it all in Donald. He was so tender and sweet. Our sex life was great. But all that's gone now.

"I don't know if it's his work or what, but Donald is so preoccupied with *his* life that he has little time for me. And nothing that I do can make Donald change. To tell you the truth, marriage has been a great disappointment, but if I give myself another chance, maybe there will be someone else for me."

Giving Up Illusions of Love

I left the restaurant feeling sad. My marriage was many years older than Gail's. I understood the pain she was feeling. I had felt it myself. After a few years our initial romance was gone. Somehow muddy tennis shoes and mashed potatoes replaced sweet music and moonlight. "A Time for Us" was no longer our song.

I felt the agony of failing to create my dream. Here was my mate, and we were not mated in the deepest sense of the word. After our honeymoon, all that I longed for seemed to vanish like steam from a boiling kettle. I liked the heat of intensity, but I couldn't seem to get the pot boiling again.

I tried to recapture the vision of marriage that I carried in my heart. Like Gail I found lots of aids to tell me how to spice up my love life and have my husband "fall in love" with me again. Not only did the secular market provide me with advice, but the Christian market did also. In fact, the more Christian books I read on how to be the perfect wife, the more depressed I became. I even took a course called "The Proverbs 31 Woman." The teacher packed her teaching with all I should be and should do. That course was almost my undoing.

Many women I knew, who had been married the same length of time as I had been, experienced marital unrest. We all compared. We all complained. We all connived. Some of us had deeper problems than others, but one thing was definitely clear: we all had illusions about love. We all lived with the Depression Vulture, and his sharp beak pecked at our emotions.

Those of us whose marriages survived seemed to go through a grief period—a giving up of the dream, the fantasy that our husbands would rescue us from all loneliness and emptiness. We came to realize that although Sir Walter Raleigh threw out his cape for his lady, he didn't throw it every time she took a step.

Mourning the death of my dream was a long, painful process. To give up my ideal, my illusion of romantic love, took time. But when I got to the other side of that dream, I could walk firmly in my reality. Yes, my husband and I needed to grow together and also separately. Our growth would continue to be a lifetime challenge. Nevertheless, our marriage had its good, solid parts.

I urged Gail to enter into the grief of her dream, but her mind was set. She went through the divorce, and she is still searching for her prince.

A Realistic Look

In his book *When Enough Is Enough*, Dr. David Augsburger explains how expectations change, mature, and unfold in marriage. He says that false hopes bedevil the early marriage.

The hope of finding the perfect partner, of achieving the perfect marriage, of basking in total acceptance, of thrilling to unbroken romance, of growing together without pain or conflict, of being understood instantly and completely, of having needs met without needing to ask. Each couple's list, though different, is embarrassingly long. Growth in covenanting a fulfilling marriage takes place in direct relationship to these hopes' demise.[1]

In other words we must give up our unrealistic hopes in order for a deeper love to emerge.

In romantic love we live out a dream—the dream we have put together from the "Cinderella myths." We daydream about *our* prince, using what we have read in magazines and books and seen on TV and movies as part of the scene. When we find the *one*, we play out that dream. We are not our real selves but the actresses in our dream. We become absorbed by and with our beloved. We passionately desire to be one spiritually, mentally, emotionally, and physically. United—truly united. So one that we will never be alone or abandoned again. We are intoxicated. Drunk on romance.

This rush of "falling in love" is wonderful and important. It gives us the courage to lower our ego walls while we explore each other. We melt together. While this is only the first step in the relationship, many women feel abandoned when the days of falling in love are replaced with the reality of each individual. We desire perfect love. Love that never fails to understand and to absorb the other's needs. It is the loss of the falling-in-love state that is often at the root of our frustration.

Karen told me her story:

"I had dreamed of the time that one man would come for me. I thought of myself as fairly sophisticated and independent. You know—the modern woman who could live with or without a man, but I was constantly getting myself ready for IT by everything I wore, everything I thought, and everything I read. Most of all I wanted to be ready sexually. I wanted to give not too much but with the promise of more to come.

"My early romances were intense but seemed to fade at a certain point. Finally, when I was twenty-six, I met Tom.

"He swept me off my feet. I was giddy. I was totally fascinated and willing to give him every bit of me. I could see a life of total romance, forever happy and peaceful. If I could have been realistic, I would have told you that my expectations of Tom were impossible. But I didn't have a rational thought in my head. I was living on high emotion.

"I wanted this love to be what I wanted so much that I denied any conflict. I simply let our problems fade away—never confronting the issues. After Tom and I married, I began pulling my head out of the sand and looking at our differences. It was so painful and frightening. I thought I wasn't in love. It took a long time and a lot of work to realize I was entering the beginning of real love. First, though, I had to let go of my false hopes."

Like most of us, Karen tried living out her dream. When everyday life problems and challenges entered the picture, she had difficulty coping. Letting go of our illusions is difficult, but it is important so that we can take the next step into love.

The Prince Has Warts

In *The Road Less Traveled*, M. Scott Peck, M.D. talks about falling in love as a false perception, an illusion. The wife wants to go shopping, the husband wants to go bowling. She wants to save money, he wants to buy a lawn mower. She wants to discuss everything, he doesn't want to talk. Little by little each individual takes back his personal space, and they "fall out of love." Peck says: "Once again they are two separate individuals. At this point they begin either to dissolve the ties of their relationship or to initiate the work of real loving.[2]

Actually the feeling of not being "in love" with your mate is what drives many women to despair. This state of despair often leads to a marriage of sad resignation or to divorce. By understanding the difference between "falling in love" and the true act of loving, we can come to terms with the love commitment of long-term marriage. We can actually embrace our prince who has warts and a few freckles.

Women who insist on continuing to search for their true love (the one who will sustain the romantic state) often fall into infidelity, or they divorce and remarry. By sheer determination some women create the myth of "honeymoon-in-loveness" in their marriage even though it no longer exists. Accepting our mates, warts and all, is an important step of love. We all want to be accepted as we really are. In order to begin accepting, we have to give up the illusions of perfection. We have to set our husbands free—and be free ourselves.

Kristin was six years older than Burt when they married. Concerned about their age difference, Kristin worked hard to look her youngest during their courtship. Months after they were married she confided, "I still wear full makeup to bed every night. I'm afraid Burt won't accept me if he really sees what I look like."

Kristin still tried to create an illusion, and the makeup symbolized that illusion. After a time she let herself be even more fully known. The makeup came off and the love deepened. They took a step into a new kind of love.

Removing our masks and revealing our true selves is risky business. We worry subconsciously that we won't be accepted; however, if we don't risk, we can never know or be known.

The Prince and Princess Redefined

OK, my prince has warts. I've said it. Now what? Now we get down to the real business of love. Love is action. A verb. Love is work. A commitment.

In Chapter 3 I wrote about the stages of friendship. Marriage has its stages too. Understanding these stages can help us as the glow of intense romance fades and is replaced by the challenge of living with another. Like the stages of friendship, in marriage we have:
- *the time of fascination* (We explore each other.)
- *the time of truth* (The myth of perfection falls apart.)
- *the time of recommitment* (We end the relationship or recommit to something new.)

Those of us who work at love go from one marriage stage to another during the lifetime of the marriage. Each stage is important; each has its own set of joys and challenges.

We actually can have different marriages with the same person. As we pass through fascination and exploration into reality, we come to a time of challenge. Will we leave the marriage or renegotiate? Will we redefine the terms of our marriage or leave?

Augsburger says that each marriage is actually three sequential marriages.

Marriage One lasts from years one to seven. These are the years of oneness in which there's fusion and confusion. The couple tries to blend into one but wrestles with the question "Which one?" Romantic fantasies dominate and the relationship is complementary. The roles of husband and wife are fixed and conflict is suppressed.

Marriage Two takes place during the eighth to fifteenth year. Separation occurs with each defining his or her other identity. The fantasies collapse. The two dependent people now forge their independence and conflict is aroused. Each tries to force the other to fulfill unrealistic expectations.

Marriage Three occurs during the fifteenth to fiftieth year. The couple reunites, each retaining a separate identity. There is a healthy sense of both "I" and "we." A deeper love forms. The couple has a realistic love of self and each other. In a lifetime there may be even Marriage Four, Five, and Six.[3]

"Last week was my fourteenth anniversary. I don't know

if there'll be a fifteenth or not!" said Bonnie. Like Bonnie, most of us get stuck in the difficulty of Marriage Two. "These past five years have been pretty horrible for Dan and me. He blames it on my going back to finish working on my college degree. He says school has separated us but, quite frankly, I have to do something for myself.

"He's what you'd call a workaholic. Always trying to get ahead. And when I complain that I want equal time with the computer, he says he's doing it all for me. So what can I say? It's terrible. Even our sex life is on a boring schedule. I thought when we married we would work toward real oneness!" Bonnie shook her head.

"You know, it's almost as if he was having an affair with his business—so I guess I decided to have an affair with my education."

Bonnie and Dan are in that stressful time of longing for the first power of eros and at the same time separating to discover themselves. This time of stretching and testing can be a frightening time, and many couples today bail out at this point. Perhaps if we better understood the importance of this adult growth for ourselves and Marriage Three, we could encourage the exploration. Committing, communicating, and compromising without being defensive can help the couple see this step as exciting. This time of personal development will eventually become the rich fertilizer for an even more fruitful marriage.

Bonnie and Dan began counseling. They didn't "feel" like they were in love anymore, but they did have fourteen irreplaceable years invested in the marriage. Over the months they came to understand that they needed to keep discovering their own gifts—still keeping each other prominently in mind. They needed to learn how to be fully independent and interdependent at the same time. They needed to learn to communicate better.

Bonnie still expected Dan to understand what she needed without telling him. Unrealistic. Dan expected Bonnie to be the adoring, waiting wife he had the first year of marriage.

Unrealistic. As they uncovered their unrealistic expectations of each other and discovered they were in a time of growth, they began the work of loving in a different and conscientious way.

One evening the counselor asked them each to list twenty ways they felt loved by the other. They exchanged lists. Then they were to do one loving thing for the other each day.

"It was such a little thing," said Bonnie, "but one morning Dan brought me a cup of coffee in bed and we talked a minute before he left for work. I felt loved all day! It made such a difference."

Bonnie and Dan redefined their marriage and hung in there through the hard part of growing instead of divorcing and looking for new partners. Both are maturing in a healthier way. They have a better understanding of the work of love. Now they look forward to developing deeper intimacy as they grow older together.

The Prince and Princess Grow Up

Lisa's hair was a crown of silver. Her face was a story written with a maze of gentle life lines. Propped on her dresser among pictures of children and grandchildren was her wedding portrait—Lisa, age twenty-two in a white satin gown with her handsome, black-haired husband, Phil, beside her. That morning I strained to see the likeness of the old woman beside me and the young, full-lipped beauty in the picture. Lisa was my grandmother.

"We're not as passionate as we used to be," she said, winking a blue eye at me. "But we love each other deeper now."

During her lifetime my grandmother told me many stories of her life. Grandpa died at ninety-four and Grandma at ninety-three. I observed the love relationship of my grandparents through their middle years into their autumn and winter.

God blessed them with seventy-one anniversaries. During their lifetime it was evident they renegotiated their marriage contract as they grew separately and together. Grandma told me of her first meeting at church with the handsome young Phil. They "fell in love" and their courting days of church socials and picnics and walks were filled with blissful dreams and stolen kisses.

She told me about their Marriage One. They struggled to explore their oneness under the heavy load of farming and living with in-laws. They soon moved into the Marriage Two.

"I wanted a new floor for the kitchen when the babies started coming," said Grandma, "and your grandpa wanted to put up a new barn. Well, we got the new barn and I was hopping mad. Next time around I got a new floor."

As time moved along, they moved along with it and the stripping force of history. War, dust bowl, failing crops, depression, war, inflation. Their personal history included children, grandchildren, great-grandchildren, and great-great-grandchildren and the joy and pain of life in between.

I went back to Kansas to visit them on the old wheat farm. I found them frail but feisty. It was a good time for me to be near them. After nine years of marriage, I wondered if Gary and I were in love anymore.

My marriage seemed more like an endurance run than a partnership. Did this mean the mystery of oneness was an illusion? We seemed to operate in separate worlds. Did this mean the marriage was over? There seemed to be an irritating unspoken conflict. Did this mean there was no chance for peace and communication? I didn't understand it, but I was in the difficult Marriage Two stage.

Watching Grandpa washing up for breakfast at the deep sink on the sunporch and Grandma pouring hot water into the brown china teapot, as they had done for so many years, gave me a solid sense of living. Sitting with their tea and toast, Grandpa covered Grandma's fragile hand with his shaky, blue-veined hand and squeezed it gently. They smiled at each other—and said grace.

I sensed they understood the mystery I was uncovering. The mystery of living an entire life with another person for better or for worse, in sickness and in health, until death do us part. The mystery of love lived out through all of love's stages.

I began to realize that as they matured they had enriched each other's life. With the commitment of being forever married they could grow and change.

Marriage Secrets

Somewhere along the line Grandpa accepted that Grandma was not only his wife but also Lisa—Lisa, who loved lilacs and fried fish. Lisa, who had strong opinions on church matters and family affairs. Lisa, who muttered in German under her breath when Aunt Ruth tried to boss her around. Somehow Grandpa learned that loving was accepting the rosebud at twenty and the fading, full-blown rose at ninety. The same woman, but a woman added to through many seasons.

My grandmother learned the same secret. Her marriage was like a river. Sometimes low from lack of rain, sometimes flooding its bank from a downpour, full of power and danger. Still, as it ran its course, the river gave incredible life.

My grandparents were no longer threatened by the surprises in each other; rather they embraced the newness along with the familiar. They had freed each other to be all each one could be. Then they had turned and given that gift of wholeness to each other. Perhaps they had had many marriages with each other in their years. Their first fragile relationship had grown and changed numerous times with the marriage being renegotiated and renewed as the anniversaries came and went. From the first enchantment of "falling in love," they had learned about "living in love."

I needed my grandmother's wisdom. "Tell me how to live married, Grandma." I blinked back a surprise rush of tears. "Sometimes it's so hard."

"Child, I guess everybody has their list, but I'd say learn to be friends and have friends with other folks too. You've got to learn to talk and not be afraid when you disagree. Just keep talking. Laughing helps. We've laughed when there's nothing to laugh about, but it seems to act like glue." Grandma paused for a minute and then smiled as she remembered something in the past.

"You've got to be tolerant! Each man has his moods and no amount of nagging is going to change him. And be honest. Your whole life's based on trust you know." She smiled again. "And love each other—with celebration. If you mix all that with prayer, you'll make it, honey."

I thought about her words and made a list in my journal:
Be friends
Communicate
Be honest
Laugh
Be tolerant and flexible
Make love
PRAY

There were items here that had almost died from neglect in my marriage. One thing was certain. I needed to work on changing myself—not Gary. And I needed to deepen my relationship with the Lord.

At the end of my stay I felt renewed. Seeing a lifetime of committed love lived out gave me hope and energy. I felt ready for recommitment to my husband. I didn't know it at the time, but I was readying for a renegotiation of marriage—for Marriage Three.

When Will My Prince Come?

One of the difficulties I had in giving up my marriage ideal and taking up the marriage work had to do with my Cinderella dream. Everyone knows the story, but where did it come from?

The story begins: Once upon a time there was a beautiful

girl who lived with her father, wicked stepmother, and two terrible stepsisters. Her name was Cinderella. Her life was unbelievably hard. No one understood her deepest longings. No one appreciated her. No one loved her. Then one night she met the Prince. They fell deeply in love. They were separated, but the Prince searched until he found her. Of course you know they married and lived happily ever after.

The story of Cinderella and similar fairy tales have gotten bad reviews lately. Some psychologists, feminists, and writers say these fairy tales teach little girls to expect a magical prince to rescue them from their miserable lives. Then, after a fairy-tale wedding, they can expect to live "happily ever after." Psychologists and others who believe in the "Cinderella Syndrome" have a point, but these stories may have an even deeper meaning.

As a storyteller, I have studied myths and fairy tales for years. Most of the great themes reappear over and over throughout ages and cultures. (The first recorded Cinderella theme is dated ninth century A.D., from China.) I believe, as Carl Jung did, that recurring themes contain archetypal symbols and stories expressing universal truths.

Why is Cinderella such a favorite? Why did my friend's little girl, Jenny, come night after night with the storybook in her hand saying, "I know it's not true, but please read Cinderella one more time"? Is it because, even when we are small children, we desire a man to sweep us off our feet into loveland?

Perhaps Cinderella symbolizes each of us—the girl whose earthly life is unbelievably hard. No one understands our deepest longings. No one deeply appreciates or knows us. No one truly loves us. We are lost. We long for a Prince to come and save us.

I believe stories like Cinderella tell us a deep truth—a truth we have missed or misunderstood. This truth emerges even in ancient fairy tales. God has implanted a longing within us for Him—the One who knows and understands us, the One who made us for Himself, the Perfect Lover.

We hold this longing within us and look for our prince to come in the form of a human mate. We hope there is someone who will:

- fully understand us
- accept us as we are
- never leave us
- set us free to be our full selves
- protect us
- provide for us
- give us a sense of identity
- fully love us
- save us
- be one with us

When *the* man comes, our passions surge. Our hearts say, "This is it!" This man will fulfill all the expectations we hold unspoken in our deepest selves. So we marry our vision, but this new husband fails. The Depression Vulture flops his wings over our marriages and shadows our lives. Our joy disappears.

The Holy Prince

There is a Holy Prince, and when we meet the Holy Prince, we find He alone understands us. He alone appreciates us. He alone knows and accepts us. He alone can save us.

We fall deeply in love with the One who loves us. And even if at times we are separated, our Prince will search for us until He finds His love. Of course, in the end we will be married and live happily ever after.

In her album "To the Bride" Anne Herring of the Second Chapter of Acts tells of her fascination with *Snow White*. As a little girl she was affected by the story. She loved to sing "Someday My Prince Will Come."

One day her older sister told Anne that she couldn't marry a prince because she didn't have royal blood. But when Anne was in her twenties, her Prince did come. She met Jesus who forgave her sins and gave her royal blood. She knew He would come for His bride on a white horse with King of Kings written on His thigh. She wrote and sang "Prince Song" in celebration of His love for her.[4]

Letting a Husband Be Human

A human husband is just that—human. He cannot be God for us. What our hearts long for, and may not recognize, is a relationship with our True Prince, Jesus Christ. He is the one who can quench our thirst. We need to drink deeply from our true Lover.

God whispers His love words to us over and over. "I have loved you with an everlasting love; therefore I have drawn you with loving-kindness" (Jer. 31:3). He talks to His own as a husband would. He says, "I will betroth you to Me forever" (Hosea 2:19). When we open ourselves to His wooing and invite Him to live in us, we become filled with an everlasting love.

Knowing who our true Beloved is allows us to look realistically at our human beloved. When our deepest needs are met, we can stop demanding the impossible perfection of another human being.

I realize that if my husband could have met all of my innermost needs, he would have become my god. I would never have gone on in my spiritual journey.

No matter how perfect my husband could be for me, ultimately he will fail me because in the end, we will be separated. One of us will die and leave the other. Only God in His loving-kindness will be with me in life and death and eternal life. He, then, is my true Prince—the Love my soul has searched for—and found.

Thinking It Through

1. What do you want in a husband—physically, emotionally, financially, spiritually?
2. What is your vision of marriage?

3. How would you define love?
4. What unrealistic expectations of marriage and a mate do you have? Where did they come from?
5. Were you disillusioned when your feelings of "in loveness" began to fade? What did you do?
6. In what ways do you accept your husband? How do you try to change him? How do you risk letting yourself be known by him?
7. In what ways can you accept the challenges of the time of fascination, the time of truth, and the time of recommitment?
8. Which "marriage" are you experiencing within your marriage right now?
9. How can you separate committed love from *feeling* in love? How do you live out committed love in your marriage?
10. God tells us through His Word of His everlasting love. Read and meditate on Isaiah 54. What does Isaiah 54:5 mean to you?

"Exult and shout for joy and do Him homage, for the wedding-day of the Lamb has come! His bride has made herself ready, and for her dress she has been given fine linen, clean and shining"

(Rev. 19:7, NEB).

Chapter Seven

CAN I BUY MY WAY?
Unrealistic Expectations of Money and Power

N ow these are my before and after pictures," said Shari, "so let me lay them out on the table in order." My friend's blue eyes danced with excitement.

"I took these heavy drapes down." She tapped her finger on the color photo. "And put up these darling pleated fabric shades. It makes all the difference in the world! I hated the floor, so we ripped it out and put in light gray tile."

I examined the pictures to get the idea. Shari has a gift for decorating. Under her direction color and fabric create beautiful magic. She held up the last picture of over-stuffed couches and Indian pots, in pastel peaches and greens and striking pastel prints. "I did the whole downstairs in a Santa Fe style. It's wonderfully comfortable!"

During Shari's three-day stay, we talked and laughed, enjoying the deep friendship we've built through the years. I hated to see her car pull out of the driveway.

When her car disappeared down the street, I banged through the back screen door and thought of throwing a load of clothes in the washer. Instead I ended up sitting at the kitchen table, feeling empty. I began to pick at the peeling lacquered finish with my fingernail. The table wasn't really an antique. Just old. And warped. I rolled my favorite blue and white mug between my palms. It was chipped. My left-over coffee was cold.

My oak chair squeaked, reminding me that all four kitchen chairs needed regluing. I eyed the rip in one of the blue-checked seat covers. I looked around the kitchen. My mind began to roll. *The cabinets. Dull! They need refinishing. Maybe a light oak stain. And a little wallpaper would perk up this kitchen. Maybe a sunshiny yellow.* Before long I was desperate to re-dress the kitchen from top to bottom.

Everything seemed old, dingy, and unbearable. I got up and ran my hands along the top of the white Formica counter. Scratches and nicks. *If only I had some money, I could really make this place cute. Get rid of some of this junk. Even this dumb, chipped cup.* With great resolve I dumped out my old coffee and pitched the cup in the garbage sack under the sink.

The next day I felt the same way. Possessed. All I could think of was redecorating room after room of my house. On my way to the grocery store, I swung the car into the Santa Ynez Wallpaper and Paint Store parking lot. I spent an hour leafing through wallpaper books and looking at matching material swatches. On the way to the bank, I stopped in at Lester's Carpets and Flooring. Running my fingers through the deep-piled carpet samples, I visualized walking barefoot across new white carpeting on our bedroom floor. What luxury! The saleswoman figured out the cost. "Let's see—carpet, padding, and labor would be. . . . " She punched some figures on her computer and showed me the cost. I paled, thanked her, grabbed my purse, and left.

What am I doing? I thought as I pulled into the bank. *We can't afford new carpet.* Standing in line, I looked at my bank balance. *I can't even afford new sheets! If only I had more money.*

Money thoughts. They flooded me all the way home. Money thoughts always had a shotgun effect on my emotions. I felt powerless. Empty. I drove home with my mind spinning. Plans. Carefully, I eased the car into the crowded garage. *If only I could hire someone to help me clear out this junk.*

I slid out of the car with my groceries. As I muscled my bags through the screen door, I noticed long scratches which the dog had inflicted in the black paint. In the kitchen I opened the door of my wheezing refrigerator and shoved in a carton of 2 percent milk on the sticky shelf. *If only I'd scrub this old machine, it would look better.* I sighed. *What we really need is a new refrigerator!* My anxiety and powerlessness took another giant growth spurt.

Suddenly, I felt a presence. A real presence. Sure enough! The Depression Vulture had flapped in with me and was laying an egg in my kitchen.

I went to a meeting the next morning, planning to leave early so I could look at wallpaper books in Santa Barbara. I greeted the women and sat near the front door so I could slip out if the agenda went on and on. As the meeting began, I tried to focus, but my mind spun off into chintz prints, rose-colored paint, and flowery area rugs.

Kerry sat across from me with her blond, pink-cheeked seven-month-old Sara playing at her feet. Baby Sara was surrounded with a fuzzy yellow duck, a busy box that snapped and buzzed, and a cloth book of ABCs in dazzling red, blue, and yellow. I watched in fascination as she discarded her beautiful toys, and crawled efficiently to something on the rug. Her treasure? A pink snapdragon that had dropped from a flower arrangement. She grasped her discovery and sat up. After examination she tasted it. Clapping her chubby little hands, she grinned until her mother cleared her mouth and sat her back in the middle of her toys. Sara soon busied herself pulling car keys and Kleenex from someone's navy blue purse.

Baby Sara's contentment poked at my discontent. Centered on her work of investigation, her interior life was focused and wonderfully simple. She didn't demand complicated, expensive toys. Her joy came from discovering life around her.

Watching little Sara I remembered my children's passion for boxes.

"Can we go to the alley?" four-year-old Steven would ask. We'd pack up two-year-old Jeff and drive behind Gilbert's Appliance Store looking for THE BIG BOX. Steven made his selection. I hauled it home in the station wagon. Through magic imagination, the box became a cave or a rocket. A ranch house or a plane. A train or a store. If Steven felt generous, his little brother could come in the box, but it wasn't long before I had to haul two BIG BOXES home from Gilbert's.

When Katherine was old enough for a BIG BOX, the boys still loved box fun. Doll house or hospital. Fishing boat or secret room. Club house. They painted boxes, cut out windows, put two or more together. When the boxes collapsed from age or accident, they flattened them and used them to slide down a hill. Nothing ever equaled a new refrigerator box to stimulate creative fun and joy. The children's boxes reminded me about simplicity's joy.

The Seduction of Things

As wonderful as simplicity is, we are lured into wanting things. Our culture teaches us that more is better. As we feel our days rushing by, we try to grab some life—often by getting as many possessions as we can. We begin to believe that if we have more, we will be happy.

How we love our stuff! Starting in our early years we collect dolls, doll houses, books, wagons, and trikes. Then we move on to skateboards, Brownie uniforms, record players, tape recorders, TVs, bikes, jewelry, and clothes. As youngsters we collect, we store, we trade, we sell, we use, we show and tell.

I heard a lot of "If only I had . . . " from my children. From early on they wanted things. TV commercials, catalogs, kid's magazines, even cereal boxes promised a treasure that would bring earth's greatest delights. I kept a chart on the refrigerator to keep track of who got the next cereal box prize. The prize never delivered the promised joy. The little

plastic doodad inside usually lasted less than a minute before
it fell apart. I often longed to dump out the cereal and give
the kids the empty box. With a little creative juice they
could have had more fun. But their passion remained. They
wanted their prizes.

As children, when we long for something, it consumes our
thoughts. How will we get it? If birthday or Christmas is too
far away, maybe we can beg for it. If that doesn't work,
maybe we'll try to work, save our money, and buy the prize
ourselves.

We forget the simple wonder of examining a pink snapdragon or pretending in a box, watching clouds change
shape, or catching fireflies in a jar. We are in pursuit of
something more wonderful. We think that *something* is whatever we don't have.

In our society teenagers are the target of billion-dollar ad-
vertising. Bombarded with pictures, words, and sound, they
are told what they *have* to wear, eat, or own in order to be
successful young people. Luxuries become necessities.
Many of them work to gain financial power to buy what they
want. We always want more.

Fifteen-year-old Shirley told this story: "I just bought a
stone-washed jean jacket. My two best friends have one just
like it. It was expensive. Really outrageous in a way, but I
wanted it more than anything. Mom said she wouldn't buy it
for me, so I started saving my baby-sitting money. Last
Wednesday I had enough money to buy it. I was thrilled to
death.

"I bought the jacket and wore it that night. I was so
happy. But you know what? Now I want the matching
skirt." Shirley shrugged her shoulders. "I wanted that jacket
more than anything. I like it, but it doesn't seem all that
important anymore. Am I always going to want something
else?"

Shirley's experience is universal. We long for *something*,
but when we get that *something*, it fills us for a brief moment
and then we want something more. Shirley asks a good ques-

tion. If she pursues the answer, perhaps she can enjoy her possessions without being possessed by them. Perhaps she will learn that accumulating things will never make her acceptable or fill her emptiness. If she searches for the answer, she will learn the secret of simplicity. She will learn that only God can deeply satisfy her. He will satisfy her, not with things, but with Himself.

Work's Wonderful Promise

Our society promises that a good job will provide us with all the security and belongingness we need. Nancy believed that the right work would solidify her future and take care of her anxieties.

The spring Nancy graduated from college, I took her to lunch. She had landed a good job and was moving to Los Angeles. "I'm glad my mom pushed me into a business major. It looks like I can make a lot more money than I could have by teaching." Nancy handed me her professional resumé and a slick brochure about her new company.

"It's not that I wouldn't like to teach. But the work's hard and the salary is so low." Nancy paused for a breath and looked directly at me. "Besides, I want a more visible profession. Corporate level management is wide open for young women."

I had known Nancy since she was twelve. When I directed the preschool, she had talked to me about becoming a teacher. After her parents divorced, family finances were precarious. Nancy felt there was never enough money. In high school she told me she was going to college to land a good job and make a big salary.

"This looks exciting!" I said, handing back the brochure. "I hope the job turns out to be what you want."

"Don't worry about me. I'm going to make good money." She slipped back to her childhood with her special twelve-year-old grin. "And that's just the beginning!" I sat smiling with my young friend, praying in my heart for her future. At twenty-two she had the exuberance of youth and a lot of unrealistic expectations.

About five years after we had that conversation, Nancy called me. She was in town and wanted to come by. No sooner had I put on the coffee than a Red Toyota XL pulled into the driveway. Dressed in a navy blue executive power suit, her red-brown hair cut in a sophisticated wedge, Nancy swung her long legs out of the car.

"I'm on my way home from a conference . . . " her words tumbled out as we hugged, "and I thought I'd come through here." Suddenly, I felt incredibly old and dowdy, wearing my baggy gray sweats and standing beside this obviously successful young beauty.

As I sliced up fruit and cheese and poured coffee, Nancy talked about her career. "Did you know I'm Assistant Director of the Human Resources now?" I listened as her life story bubbled out. She took a sip of coffee, then to my surprise, she looked up with tear-filled eyes.

"Tell me what's wrong," Nancy said. "I have all this and I'm not happy. Really, the job is just a job. I keep thinking of it as a stepping-stone, but I'm not sure stepping up is going to give me what I want."

We talked about the power of money and work—the politics, the challenges, women in corporations, ambitious career dreams. "I'm not sure I want to sell my soul," said Nancy, "but to make it big I really have to devote myself 110 percent to the company."

"What do you want in your life?" I asked.

"It's more than money—but I guess I'm hooked on the money this job brings in. And someday I want to get married, maybe have a child. But right now I have car payments, insurance, rent. I'd like to buy a place of my own." Nancy shook her head. "I used to know exactly what would make me happy, but now I'm not so sure."

Nancy believed if she built career security, she would find happiness. The Depression Vulture, hissing that she needed more and more, encouraged her credit card purchases, loans, and high style of life. Now she felt trapped—and, most important, her present lifestyle clashed with her deeper Christian values.

"I just can't sort out what the Bible says about if you have two coats and your brother has none, give him one of yours. I have to look good for my work, but I'm beginning to feel uneasy about having so much."

Work's Surprising Challenge

I thought a lot about Nancy after she left. I knew that unless she began choosing her own values and living by them, she would probably be swept away by the powerful influences of our culture.

Her questions stimulated questions of my own—old unresolved, complex questions of how to live in my culture and be God's person. In the world but not of it. My obsessions with possessions and buying power were different from Nancy's, but they existed.

We need money to live, to provide the basics of food, clothes, and shelter. A life of poverty without the basic necessities is misery. The Bible tells us to work to provide for ourselves. It also admonishes us to share with those who cannot work. We get no heavenly brownie points for living without the basics.

Whether single or married, women in today's society feel pressured to have a professional life outside the home. The world of work is open to women in almost every field. Serving as doctors, ministers, lawyers, engineers, corporate executives, professors, editors-in-chief, and stockbrokers, women are making their mark and have the power to change things. However, as exhilarating as work in a woman's life can be, it is only part of her life. Especially if she is a wife and mother.

Cynthia, a corporate real-estate manager, shared her story with me. "I made a career change and got lucky," she explained. "I make a good salary and have parlayed it into more. I love my work! I'm what you'd call a workaholic. A sixty-hour week is usual for me.

"I knew people who could team up with me and get things accomplished, not only professionally, but also in the larger community." Cynthia stood up and looked out the window.

"Let me tell you, there's a trade-off. The ads show a woman working hard, doing aerobics, serving gourmet meals, looking beautiful, being the perfect lover, wife, and mother. Listen, no woman can have it all. I know. I tried it all—and lost.

"After a bout with breast cancer, I took stock of my life. Without my work my life wasn't worth a plugged nickel. I realized I worked to block out the pain of my divorce. I'm making some big life changes now. I ran out of ME power and turned to Someone bigger."

Finding a balance of work, money, and power as God's person is a great challenge. Discovering that the power of work and money is a gift to be used for good, we can become thankful stewards. Manna must be handled with care. If we store it up out of selfishness or fear, we may find worms in our stockpile.

Paul writes to Timothy, saying:

> Godliness with contentment is great gain. For we brought nothing into the world, and we can take nothing out of it. But if we have food and clothing, we will be content with that. People who want to get rich fall into temptation and a trap and into many foolish and harmful desires that plunge men into ruin and destruction. For the love of money is a root of all kinds of evil. Some people, eager for money, have wandered from the faith and pierced themselves with many griefs (1 Tim. 6:6-10, NIV).

Cynthia is learning to put her hope, not in wealth, but in God. She has gained security far beyond her big paycheck.

The Puzzle of Money

America's standard of living has risen to an all-time high. Our country's basics can be backbreaking. Homes, cars, hospital insurance, life insurance, dishwashers, washers, dryers, garbage disposals, TVs, stereos, telephones, and answering machines. We think of these things not as luxuries but as necessities.

Parents give everything they can to their children. Good medical care. The best daycare and preschools. Music and dance lessons. Soccer, basketball, baseball leagues. Scouting. 4-H. Camp. College. All these cost money. Plenty of money.

Many of us long to change our way of living. Like Nancy, an uneasy feeling stirs within us concerning the teaching of our faith and our use of money. It's like the wicked stepsister trying on the glass slipper. No matter how we cram our lifestyle into the Gospel teaching, it just doesn't fit. But we don't know how to get off the merry-go-round.

We ride the merry-go-round, hoping for more job power and higher pay. We hope our jobs have meaning beyond the money. We read *Working Woman* magazine to learn how to rewrite our resumé, handle our bosses, and cook a meal in five minutes. We press for more energy and more time. As my friend Alice said, "I could do it all if I just had a wife."

We see ourselves and our children wrapped up in wants, searching for the right *things* to fill up vague longings, to settle insecurities, to quiet the nagging whispering of the Vulture saying, "You owe it to yourself." Still, nothing completely satisfies.

We are cautioned in Proverbs to desire wisdom above riches. Ecclesiastes tells us, "Whoever loves money never has money enough" (Ecc. 5:10, NIV). But we look at our monthly bills and we wonder. What's the way out?

Money Secrets

The money subject is a secret (sacred to some), red-hot subject. A forbidden subject, one's money power is held close to one's chest. But Jesus talked openly about money. The Gospel shows Him constantly bringing money into focus so that we can defuse its power and deal with its hidden mystery.

As His kingdom people, we can stop letting money use us and learn to use money; we can stop letting our work use us and learn to work for better life. If we harness work and money, we can use them for good. But this won't happen magically. We will have to think clearly, plan, and take action to master the dark side of money and work.

Money can become an obsession. Money schemes become our life's focus and rival our God. Jesus warned us about mammon. He knew the dangers involved and the seduction of its power. He understood the way for us to bridle this power for good, and He showed us the way.

Paul's caution to the beloved that "the *love* of money is a root of all kinds of evil" shakes us up. So, we ask, should we give it all away? Foster, in *Money, Sex and Power*, writes:

> Believers who are rightly taught and disciplined are enabled to hold possessions without corruption and use them for the greater purposes of the Kingdom of God.
>
> The truth is that total divestiture is usually a very poor way to help the poor. Certainly it is vastly inferior to the proper management and use of resources. How much better to have wealth and resources in the hands of those who are properly disciplined and informed by a Christian world view than to abandon these things to the servants of mammon![1]

Remembering to worship God instead of the power and prestige of money and work is essential because money and work are temporary. Under God's tutelage we can harness the power of greed and drive it into good works.

Those who are blessed with money have opportunities and challenges, for who better to invest their talents and make money than kingdom builders who, under the Lord's direction, can do His business of feeding the hungry, employing the unemployed, sponsoring missionaries, building colleges, retirement homes, hospitals, and child centers? Who better than His people to take leadership roles in government, business, schools, and medicine!

We must break the money secrets we cling to. We can find help among Christian sisters and brothers with whom (without moralistic, didactic answers) we can lovingly work through our money, work, and power issues.

• We can learn in Christian community, as Paul learned, to be content with much or with little.

• We can work through to the good side of power by confronting our fears and our unrealistic expectations of money.

•We can study the Gospels about money and possessions, discuss the Word together, and translate it into action.

• We can pray for each other as we learn to live as Jesus lived.

• We can encourage each other, instead of loving money and using people, to use money and love people.

• We can pray for each other's work decisions and decisions at work.

• We can learn to joyfully give away money, giving good power to those in need.

• We can treat each other as equals in the Christian community, for money has no place in preferences of people.

As we grapple with possessions, work, and money issues, we can wade through the questions together: Should I stay home with my children or work? Do we need the money for necessities or for luxuries? Do the things I want really add quality to my life when I finally have them? Can I successfully work and raise my family? Is my career meaningful? Is our product or service good for humanity? Should I make a job change? Has work or money become my god?

Dedicating our labor to God and listening for His direction, we can learn and live in the good power of work and money.

The Adventure of Simplicity

A certain simplicity, which is foreign to most of us, comes from walking in Christ. It comes from trusting that God is involved in our life and is ready to provide. The writer of Hebrews tells us, "Keep your life free from love of money, and be content with what you have; for He has said, 'I will never fail you nor forsake you' " (Heb. 13:5, RSV). What we have comes through His grace and our cooperation.

Because we trust in the power of things, work, and money more than in God to fill our deepest needs, we get sucked into the bondage of accumulation. There is never enough. That hunger for more rages.

As our spiritual life matures, we begin to understand that "He who trusts in his riches will fall, but the righteous will flourish like the green leaf" (Prov. 11:28). Our unrealistic expectations of the things of this world go flat . . . they can never satisfy.

Those who have experienced the true filling of Christ say there is a way to be satisfied. They challenge us to try the simplicity of an interior life in God.

Living in inward reality of simplicity, says Foster, will cause outward expressions of simplicity. He suggests:

- Buy things for usefulness not prestige.
- Reject buying anything that causes an addiction so we can live in freedom.
- Develop the habit of giving things away for the joy of it.
- Learn to enjoy things without having to possess them.
- Enjoy God's creation.
- Be careful of America's plan of "buy now, pay later."
- Speak in honesty and truth, letting our yes be yes and our no be no.
- Reject those things that oppress others.
- Keep away from anything that would draw us away from seeking first the kingdom of God.[2]

Oswald Chambers writes about this difficult issue.

"But seek ye first the kingdom of God, and His righteousness; and all these things shall be added unto you." Matthew vi, 33.

Immediately we look at these words of Jesus, we find them the most revolutionary statements human ears ever listened to. "Seek ye *first* the kingdom of God." We argue in exactly the opposite way, even the most spiritually-minded of us—"But I *must* live; I *must* make so much money; I *must* be clothed; I *must* be fed." The great concern of our lives is not the kingdom of God, but how we are to fit ourselves to live. Jesus reverses the order: Get rightly related to God first, maintain that as the great care of your life, and never put the concern of your care on other things.

"Take no thought for your life . . . " Our Lord points out the utter unreasonableness from His standpoint of being so anxious over the means of living. Jesus is not saying that the man who takes thought for nothing is blessed—that man is a fool. Jesus taught that a disciple has to make his relationship to God the dominating concentration of his life, and to be carefully careless about everything else in comparison to that. Jesus is saying—"Don't make the ruling factor of your life what you shall eat and what you shall drink, but be concentrated absolutely on God." Some people are careless over what they eat and drink and they suffer for it; they are careless about what they wear, and they look as they have no business to look; they are careless about their earthly affairs, and God holds them responsible. Jesus is saying that the great care of life is to put the relationship to God first, and everything else second.[3]

Life's Gifts

We came into this world with nothing and will go out with nothing—except our relationship to God. Like Adam and Eve, we think we need more than God. Complicating our lives with more and more, we are never satisfied. And even though we protect it, hide it, invest it, use it, and hoard it, we are never completely secure. Calamity can appear and throw his black cloak over anyone at anytime. The power of work and wealth bring only temporary pleasures. They can vanish in an instant. It is foolish to stake our lives on the things of this world.

I learned this lesson with a friend. One afternoon when I was still churning over completely redoing my house, I answered the soft knock on the back door. Nina looked at me with red-rimmed, puffy eyes. "You have a minute?" she asked. I wiped the last of breakfast jam off the kitchen table and we sat down.

"I can't believe it. The bank called this morning. We didn't get the loan." Nina's voice fell to a whisper. "I really thought somehow we'd pull it off. Somehow . . . "

I took her hand and sat in silence. What could I say? I knew this meant bankruptcy for Nina and her husband Pete. The first time she shared their financial problems, I was shocked. She seemed so put together. She had all the right credentials to be financially safe forever. MBA from Stanford. A career, a husband, and three achieving children. Nina and Pete built a good business, were active in church, and belonged to civic groups. Their large gracious home spoke of success. Smart investments brought them more and more money—until this last venture. They gambled and lost.

Finally, I broke the silence. "Will you lose your house?"

"I don't know exactly what will happen, but I do know one thing." Nina's words came painfully slow. "I really got off on the wrong track. This thing is going to force me to grow. We'll survive. But my direction is going to be different from now on. I told Pete that I've got to get back to the basics and find some peace."

As always I was amazed at Nina's raw honesty. I gave her a long hug and she left me—deep in thought. Her words rattled in my mind. *Back to the basics.*

Back to basics. Back to peace. I knew what Nina needed.

I knew what I needed—to be in the world but not of it. I needed to feed the gnawing hunger in me, not with the things of this world, but with the Bread of Life.

I too had lost my focus. I needed simplicity—the simplicity that comes from centering in Jesus. I needed once again to reorder my thinking concerning the power of money, work, and things. Rolling through my mind came His words, "For where your treasure is, there will your heart be also" (Matt. 6:21, NIV). My heart was treasuring things. It had forgotten to treasure Him. I opened the Word and began to read.

The late afternoon sun warmed my back as I closed my worn Bible. I rubbed my hand across my warped kitchen table. I glanced at my humming old refrigerator covered with family photos and notes and I smiled. The kitchen seemed like a familiar friend.

Suddenly, I realized my peace. The anxiety over paint, wallpaper, and carpet had disappeared like white dandelion fluff in a wind. I was deeply satisfied with my Father. The Depression Vulture fell off his perch. My contentment was more than he could stand.

Thinking It Through

1. Are you ever obsessed with thoughts about money? What triggers these thoughts?
2. What was the last *thing* you really wanted? How long did it make you happy?
3. List the luxuries that have grown to be your necessities.
4. Do your possessions possess you? What do you do and how do you feel when you lose or ruin something you love.
5. How does money give you a sense of power?
6. What is the dark side of money for you? What is the light side of money for you?
7. Do you ever feel you have enough money? How much is enough?

8. Whom do you talk honestly with about money? What things concerning money and work could you pray about?
9. How do you seek power in your job?
10. List ways you can have more of a servant attitude with work and money.
11. In what ways do you trust the power and prestige of money and work? How could they fail you?
12. Is the Lord calling you to a simpler lifestyle? What things can you do to simplify?
13. What are your unrealistic expectations of work, money, and things?

"Faith by itself, if it is not accompanied by actions, is dead"
(James 2:17, NIV).

Chapter Eight

DOES BABY LOVE MOMMY?
Unrealistic Expectations of Mothering and Children

A piercing howl echoed down the hall as two-and-a-half-year-old Shelley ran from her bedroom on chubby legs and collapsed in her mother's lap.

She held her tiny arm aloft. "He bites. He bites," she wailed. Crocodile tears splashed down her round red cheeks.

Both Mickey and I examined the arm. Sure enough, right above her dimpled elbow was the unmistakable mark of a set of small piercing teeth. Mickey put an ice pack on her baby. My blood boiling, I marched down the hall to confront the baby's adversary—my two-and-a-half-year-old son.

"What have you done, Steven? You hurt Shelley. You hurt her very badly!" Steven promptly fell on the floor like a rock. I snatched him up and carried him to look at Shelley's wound. She was nestled in her mother's arms sucking her fat little thumb between pitiful sobs and shudders. Mickey winked at me, trying to say Shelley was all right. But it wasn't all right.

"Now look at that," I said firmly, standing him in front of the wailing child. "You bit Shelley and made her cry." I pointed at the bite, and Shelley held out her arm with great drama. "Even if you get very angry, you must not bite. Now say you're sorry."

"NO!" said Steven, stomping his little bare foot hard.
"NO!"

I blinked back my own tears. *This has been a terrible, horrible, no-good day.*

"OK, Steven, time out. Sit right here." I lifted my stiff two-and-a-half-year-old to his designated "time out" chair and made him sit. He started to bawl. Turning my back to him, I wiped away my hot tears with the palm of my hand.

The Mothering Myth

Having children was *supposed* to be fun. In our early twenties Mickey and I waited out our first pregnancies together, sharing hopes and dreams of future mothering. I felt secure in my ability to mother. Kids and I always got along. I could coax the most fearful child into my lap when I baby-sat or into the water when I taught swimming. Yes, motherhood would be wonderful—a future filled with tender times of loving and being loved. However, I didn't make room in my mind for the difficult challenges of parenting.

For years I built up unrealistic expectations of being a mother. I believed that if I provided the right loving environment for my little one, everything would be beautiful. On the few challenging days, all I would need was additional patience and understanding to get mother and child back on track.

Mickey and I watched our tummies expand, wrestled with our weight, traded maternity clothes, went to each other's baby showers, waited, and at the end, waddled together. Nine months seemed like forever.

The phone jarred me from my nap one September afternoon. "We have a baby girl." Full of tears and awe, Bill's husky voice rushed through the phone. "She's a little early but just perfect! She looks like a baby robin."

As soon as Mickey came home from the hospital, I held six-pound Shelley on my full belly. Peering at her tiny pink face and crop of soft blond fuzz, I counted her fingers, looked at the v of her top lip, smelled her baby skin, and felt her breath on my face as she slept. An angel. This is how it was going to be. Excitement pulsed through my body, and I felt my baby shift his body. *He's as anxious as I am*, I thought.

"How was the delivery?" I asked, watching Mickey nurse Shelley.

"The doctors said I did fine for a first baby, but my stitches hurt like the very devil." My eyes fixed on the baby as she made wonderful sucking and breathing sounds. "Did you know she's already sleeping five to six hours at night?" said Mickey.

I should have known that not all babies were like Shelley. I soon found out.

On October 1, with Gary beside me, our six-and-one-half-pound Steven made his debut—red, screaming, and with a black eye. Already mad about not being in control, he began to take over.

From a long labor and tough delivery I was both exhausted and euphoric. Through the birthing pain and a child erupting from my body into earth life, I connected with all the rest of humanity in a primordial way. God had let me experience the most creative act in the universe. And I would go on creating by being the perfect mother for my son.

The first time I put him to my breast to nurse, I thought all my dreams had come true. But baby Steven didn't snuggle down against my skin. He stiffened his little body and then chomped down and pulled for all he was worth. His tiny fist kneaded me like a baby mountain lion. Nursing hurt. Both nipples broke open and bled. Steven howled and I cried. He began to gain weight before we left the hospital, but my Madonna and child myth was ending.

More Mothering Reality

Gary pulled our VW carefully away from the curb of the hospital and drove his precious cargo home. During my hospital stay, a hard October frost had changed the whole outside world from green into vibrant reds and yellows. I knew that my whole world inside had changed too.

Once home we took the baby into his waiting nursery, unbundled him, and looked him over. Steven cried with indignation.

"Let's try a new diaper," said Gary. While the new father unpinned the diaper, grabbed washcloth, baby lotion, and new diaper, Steven promptly sprayed us and his nursery.

The first month Steven ate every three hours. Many days I felt exhausted and crabby. My mood swings drifted from delight to depression. Things went from bad to worse when Mickey called to tell me Shelley was sleeping through the night. "Maybe you don't have enough milk," she said. I sat down gently on my rubber ring and cried. What was I doing wrong?

Perfection: The Preconceived Dream

Almost every woman thinks about being a mother. Some fear the corruption and pollution or overpopulation of the world and decide against mothering. Some fear the responsibility of a child. However, for most females being a mother is part of fulfilling womanhood.

As we grow up, we consciously and unconsciously try on the role of motherhood. We practice by mothering our dolls, our pets, and our playmates. We watch TV mothers on "The Cosby Show" and "Family Ties." We observe other women mothering and learn. We live with our own mothers and learn. For better or worse, our motherhood myths begin to take shape.

The strange thing is that few of us think about the difficulties of motherhood. We veil our minds from the heartache and challenges, saying, "That will never happen to me." Somehow we build an illusion of control. We can, we fantasize, be in control of our children, ourselves, and our world.

Pam, a young mother of two, shared this with me: "I don't

understand what happened. My dreams came true when I had a baby boy and then a girl. But to tell you the truth, it's not like I had imagined. I thought my kids would be like little dolls. I could dress them up and show them off. But sometimes they're a real pain in the neck, and I can't wait to get them to bed. A lot of the time I feel like a failure as a mother. I guess I want my kids to be too perfect."

Perfectionism is a theme that runs through our unrealistic expectations of motherhood and children. When we daydream, we think of stuffing stockings at Christmas, making hot chocolate on a rainy afternoon, reading books together by the fire, and picnicking by the lake. We all see ourselves as the perfect mother with the perfect child. When our children throw a royal temper tantrum in the grocery store, start a fire in the backyard, or flunk a math class, we mothers feel threatened. We have a hard time accepting the fact that our kids aren't perfect. We have an even harder time accepting the fact that we aren't perfect mothers, so we try to control even more.

Reality shatters our dreams. We find dirty socks under the bed, vomit on the carpet, and gum in their hair. Pam said it well when she found out she was expecting baby number three. "I thought all this was supposed to be fun. It's not! A lot of it is just hard work without a break."

In our mother-heart we long for someone to love, but even more—someone to love us. So we have a child. We dream we can perfectly love and provide for our baby. In return he will be so bonded to us that his love will fill that empty place within us, and we will have joy.

This desire to be nurtured is widespread. After interviewing 1,100 women, Louis Genevie, Ph.D., and Eva Margolies reported in their book *Motherhood Report* that most women wanted to have a child to be nurtured themselves rather than to nurture. The opportunity to mother offered a chance to relive their childhood in a more perfect way. "This desire led most women to envision motherhood in idealistic, and often unrealistic, terms. What women often seem to mean

when they say, 'I want a child,' is 'I want a perfect child.' "¹
About 70 percent of the women of all ages and educational
background had unrealistic fantasies of romance and/or fantasies of perfect family, mother, child.

It seems what most of us fail to put into the mothering
equation is a whole lot of reality. Pediatrician Dr. T. Berry
Brazelton says:

> Everyone who holds a new baby falls in love. But while
> falling in love is easy, staying in love takes commit-
> ment. A newborn demands an inordinate amount of
> time and energy. He needs to be fed, changed, cud-
> dled, carried and played with over endless 24-hour peri-
> ods. He is likely to cry inconsolably every evening for
> the first 12 weeks. Much of the time his depressed,
> frightened parents are at a loss about what to do for
> him.²

When you expected only angels in the nursery, it is quite a
shock to find the Depression Vulture perched on the end of
your crying baby's crib—but sometimes it happens.

Expecting Reality

By expecting reality we can better prepare ourselves for
motherhood. We need to know that:

● Mothering is both wonderful and difficult.

● Mothering requires a long-term commitment of energy
and time to create a good experience, so don't rush into
motherhood until you are ready.

● Mothering is done best with a supportive father, so find
a husband who will work at being a good, loving parent.

● Mothering can rob your marriage as well as add to it, so
you must jealously guard and work to strengthen your relationship with your husband.

● Mothering requires a maturing, consistent love and patience. This takes self-giving work.

- Mothering is a risk because each child may bring not only special gifts but also difficult challenges.
- Mothering is only one part of being a woman, so you must continue to grow as a whole person.
- Mothering requires wisdom and love and support to succeed, and forgiveness when you fail, so you must stay in constant contact with God.

Supermom—Superkid

"What gets me," said twenty-nine-year-old Susie, "is that it's not enough to be a mom. I've got to be a SUPERMOM and have a SUPERKID." She nodded her red head toward her three-year-old. "The whole world is telling me that David's got to play Suzuki violin, take swimming lessons, and learn to read before kindergarten. AND I've got to see to it that it happens. My mother says the whole thing is ridiculous, but you know what—the pressure's really out there."

Susie is right. Our fast-paced, high-pressured culture presents 1,001 ways to produce the perfect child. Trying to be the perfect mother sucks us into the pressure. Often we feel guilty when we try to pull back to a simpler family lifestyle. We are afraid we might fail our child if she misses being in any of the clubs or classes. We feel guilty unless our quality time is filled with trips to the museum and intimate talks to make every second meaningful.

Being a perfect parent is impossible. Trying to be perfect only gives us another opportunity to fail. Supermom is a mythical creature who has eyes so powerful she can see into the future, hands so quick she can make a bear costume while cooking for six, a heart so tough she doesn't cry and so tender she does, legs so strong she can stand all day working and stand all night cheering the kid's football team, a brain so gifted she understands her child's every need, a mouth so disciplined she always knows when to speak pearls of wisdom and when to shut up.

Dr. Brazelton says, "Understand that there is no perfect

way to be a parent. The myth of the supermom serves no real purpose except to increase the parent's guilt."[3]

Letting go of the supermom image helps us let go of unrealistic expectations of mothering. Being perfect is impossible. Only God is the perfect parent. If we look to Him, He will forgive our failures, counsel us with His wisdom, and guide our parenting. We can find the nurturing we need from Him instead of from our children. In Him we can find the consistent intimacy and the loving-kindness we long for.

Real Mothers—Real Children

"Sometimes I'm so disappointed with myself," said Gerrie, mother of three children. "Some days I'm really on top of things. But other days the kids drive me crazy. Just last week the kids had a school holiday, and I decided to spend the whole day just *being* with them. I planned a great day at the beach, but after I rearranged my schedule, packed the lunches, unearthed the beach gear, and got the boys ready, Becky, who's twelve, decided she didn't want to go."

Gerrie threw up her hands. "I lost it! I gave her a lecture that would skin a cat, telling her how thoughtless she was. The truth is that she had ruined my plans and I was disappointed. Becky and I are very different. I love to be outdoors and involved with sports. Her idea of fun is to curl up alone with a good book. I thought my daughter would be like me. You know, a female companion."

Psalm 127 says, "Children are a gift of the LORD" (v. 3). Often we expect these little gifts to be just like us. We have the challenge of raising a human being, the most significant of God's creatures. Even though we feel, as a mother, that our child is bone of our bone, flesh of our flesh, each child is formed uniquely by God in our womb. Each child is different from all other human beings. It is this difference that brings us joy and sometimes perplexing grief as we try to understand him.

The child's task of separating from mother into his

uniqueness often causes pain. Establishing his separateness was what my two-and-a-half-year-old Steven did by shouting "No" and stomping his little foot. I felt responsible for the biting incident and his defiance—as if *I* had actually acted this way myself. The extra ache in my heart came from not understanding the separation process. Becky's independence broke across her mother's lovely plan and her desire for closeness. Gerrie felt personally rejected because Becky was separating.

The business of healthy separating begins in toddlerhood, usually peaks in adolescence, and finishes in young adulthood. A mother's chief goal is to raise an independent adult, but that task doesn't fit well into the myth of peaceful, joyful mothering. When independence and rejection raise their jarring heads, mother labor and love can seem worthless.

Some children and mothers go through life fairly easily; others do not. A great deal of this depends on the God-given temperament and personality you and your child have inherited.

"Becky and I have so much trouble getting along. Some days everything she does irritates me, and I really feel guilty," said Gerrie. "I get along better with my son, Jimmy. He's so easygoing. Since I've realized Becky has a high-strung personality and needs a lot of time alone, things have been better for both of us. It's been hard to accept that we are so different."

In *The Motherhood Report* hundreds of women cited temperament as a basic factor affecting the mother-child relationship. The implication is: "It is as much the child who makes the mother as it is the mother who makes the child."[4] The easygoing, cheerful, adaptable, affectionate child makes it easier for a mother to feel good about her mothering. The baby who is a poor sleeper and eater, moody, stubborn, shy, and unaffectionate strains the mother-child relationship from the start. Children are supposed to be compliant and well-behaved. When they are not, the mother suffers.

All children bring us to our knees before the Lord. Children who differ from us or who have difficult personality traits put us in God's lap. When I accept my children as separate individuals from me, when I realize I don't own them but they are on loan, when I see they have come through me but are *not* me, then I can let go of my unrealistic expectations of them and me.

Once I realize my children have been uniquely formed in my womb and are not carbon copies of me, then I can follow the wisdom of Proverbs: "Train up a child in the way he should go and even when he is old he will not depart from it" (Prov. 22:6). The original Hebrew text suggests training up a child according to his or her bent. This means we must observe our children, to see who God has made and to discover the gifts God has given them. Then we need to nurture those gifts.

As I let go of my unrealistic expectations of Steven and examined who he was as he unfolded, our relationship changed. I realized he was responsible for his emotions and actions. I was responsible to love, guide, discipline, and accept him. To train him up in the way *he* should go. As I freed Steven to become himself, I too became free in my role as his mother.

Trying to make our children into perfect cutout dolls will have a devastating effect on both mother and child. By looking around us at faces, skin color, and shape, we observe our physical differences. It is also true that He has made us different emotionally and mentally for His own purposes. It is God's intention to create variety in His beloved sons and daughters, and so we too experience variety in our sons and daughters.

Mother Forever
Of all loves, the experience of mother love is unduplicated. Although we often fall short of our mothering goals, mother love usually remains powerful. Even if we are on our death

bed, if we need to protect our young, we rise up.

This love begins even before the baby is born. Once conception takes place in our womb, we are part of the process and out of control of the outcome. Our child may be a genius or retarded, beautiful or plain, quiet or outgoing, athletic or placid. A mother's job is to love, protect, and raise her child no matter what he is like.

In most realms of life we have options. If we don't like the material we are working with or the way things are turning out, we can throw it out and start over. In mothering, our child is our child—forever—and cannot be discarded. A mother must work with this offspring to bring about her best good. Because of this, a woman is forced to mature and develop in ways she never would if left to her own devices. (It is sad to note that some women do throw away their children by abusing and abandoning them physically and mentally. In these cases usually the parent has never been nurtured herself. Her destructive parenting, her lack of parenting, comes from deep unfulfilled need.)

The gift of a child, particularly a difficult child, makes a woman aware of all her limitations. Her original dream of a baby to love and be loved by is shattered. Because being a mother is forever, she learns something profound about the commitment of love. In motherhood we experience a life of love as a mixture of joy and grief.

Phyllis is a mother of two daughters and three sons. She told me her story. "I was the oldest child in a family of six, and my mother was so overwhelmed with everything that I didn't get much affection. I had a lot of experience with young kids, so I felt confident about raising a family. And I would do it well!" She looked away, remembering.

"My first four children were born by the time I was thirty-three. I'm not sure what I was trying to prove, but with my high energy and good organization, boy, did I run a tight ship! Oh, we had our rough times, but basically the children were compliant, accomplished kids. Secretly, I felt very proud of the way things were going, and sort of puffed up when my friends asked me how I did it.

"When I was forty-one, Danny was born." Phyllis' bottom lip trembled. She lifted her small chin and continued. "When the doctor told me he had Down's syndrome, I was devastated.

"The other children accepted Danny right away, and my husband made his peace with the situation. But I just couldn't stand it. I tried to hide my feelings. I felt so ashamed. So fearful of the future. The truth is I was embarrassed at having an imperfect child.

"Then for a long time I denied that Danny wouldn't be OK. I blocked my anxiety by thinking that if I got the right resources and gave him extra stimulation, he would be normal. But inside I grew more and more angry at God.

"I remember changing Danny one morning after the other children left for school. I looked at his little face with the wide set eyes and flat nose. Grabbing him out of bed and hugging him close, I sobbed, 'God, why did You do this to me?' For months I suffered such deep depression that I shut the rest of my family out.

"Finally, the grief began to lift as God helped me accept Danny. Danny's nineteen now. Through the years he's brought me to my knees and kept me there. Like my other children, he's given me both sadness and joy. And as hard as it has been sometimes, I can't imagine my life without his special love and affection. The Lord used Danny to deepen me."

Mothers who raise children with physical, mental, and emotional problems have the greatest challenge of all. Sometimes the child is unable to give the mother any love, and she must choose to mother because of her commitment.

Not all women can mother difficult children. Each situation is different. Some mothers, doing their best, still lack the physical or emotional coping skills to adequately face the needs of a special child. Some mothers must be strong enough to let their children be institutionalized—for the child's sake and the sake of the family.

The mothers who walk through the valleys with difficult children must draw on the deep wells of God's love and wisdom in order to grow in the painful places of their mothering life. And they need us to walk beside them.

Letting Go and Setting Free
In the end, the object of motherhood is to set our children free. Through the years we learn that our children cannot give us the feeling of security. We must give that to them. They cannot love us with unconditional love. We must give that to them. They cannot fill the deep, empty hole within us. Only God can answer that need in either of us. With God's help we can only do our best and set them free.

When our children were teenagers, Bev and I used to take long walks to recapture our sanity. Those were the days of forbidden motorcycle rides, the first driver's licenses, first dates, and crazy surprises. As we walked together, we talked about our wild lives with our teens. We discovered neither of us had any hot water left after their showers. We discovered our teens needed three towels to dry their bodies, never had clean gym shorts, and would die on the spot if they ever ate cafeteria food. The ups and downs of our lives were similar and our laughter kept us afloat.

Mothering teens has its particular set of challenges. Bev and I felt the pressure of saying no to our teens. Sometimes our noes were strongly protested. It was obvious that (for a while at least) we would not win a popularity contest with our kids.

As we hiked along one morning, Bev said something that helped me. "You know, we feel responsible for other people's emotions—like keeping the family happy. If the kids are happy, we're happy. Well, you sure can't do that with teenagers. It's their job to feel miserable!" I laughed in agreement, but later I thought about what she said.

Somehow mothers are given the unspoken burden of making the family happy. What an unrealistic expectation! That unrealistic expectation is the Thief of the joy we *can* have.

Each of us is responsible only for our own emotions. I realized that day too that my children were not responsible for my happiness either. If my teens were having a rough time, it was their rough time—not mine. We are responsible to mother, to guide, love, comfort, and listen. But ultimately, they are responsible for themselves and their feelings. We can still choose to have joy even if they don't have a date for the prom.

As we hand them the responsibility for their lives, we both take risks. They fail. We fail. Still, we learn from failure and go on. After all, that is the way we all grow and mature. If we cling to perfectionism, we will believe that our kids and ourselves must be strong, good, right, and perfect all the time. Every time you open the door to your teenager's disheveled bedroom the Depression Vulture, who is nesting in the unmade bed, will buzz your head.

In a healthy teenager's life there is usually enough friction between himself and his mother for both to finally let go. The stage is set. The time seems premature—but nature's pressures are there. So we launch our big baby bird into stages of freedom.

Setting a child free means:

- to allow learning from natural consequences, *not to rescue from problems*
- to care about, *not to care for*
- to support, *not to fix*
- to change myself, *not to change another*
- to build up another, *not to tear down*
- to talk to, *not talk at*
- to control myself, *not to control another*
- to live my life, *not live through another*
- to become flexible, *not to stay rigid*
- to live in the present, *not to live in the past*
- to hope for the best, *not to hang on to the worst*
- to live in love, *not to live in fear*
- to let go and *let God.*[5]

Mothers and Their Adult Children

When we are actively mothering, we sometimes wonder what it would be like to sleep through the night or take a bath in peace. Suddenly it happens. Our children grow up and leave home.

For some of us the departure stage is a difficult process. We miss our children. Our life role must be redefined. We feel uneasy. For most of us, even though it is an adjustment, the empty nest offers us freedom to pursue new interests. We feel excited!

As our young adult children fly off, we cheer when they soar through the clouds and cry when they crash and burn. When things go well for our adult children, we feel rewarded. When they don't, we sit in the shadow of the hovering Depression Vulture asking, "Where did I go wrong?"

Being unique people, our children may or may not make choices we might make. Their ways may differ from our way. However, as we hand them the right to manage their own lives, the right to grow from success and failures, we allow them to experience the fullness of adulthood.

By accepting our adult child's right to live her own life, we have a chance to become adult friends. Even if we never embrace her total lifestyle.

As we accept our child with her strengths and weaknesses and let go of our perfect dream child, she can better emerge into herself. We celebrate together the high moments of high school and college graduations, new jobs, engagements, weddings, and births of our grandchildren. We share the valleys of job losses, marital struggles, sickness, accidents, and deaths. But we don't try to fix. We don't try to change. We pray.

Ruth and her husband gave their daughter Monica a grand wedding with all the trimmings. Ruth was proud of their future son-in-law. "He seemed to be perfect," Ruth explained. "John was a lawyer, good-looking, and a Christian. He was the Prince Charming I'd dreamed of for Monica.

"When the marriage collapsed three years later, I was devastated. I felt so angry at my daughter that communication between us fell apart. When I tried to talk with her, she shut me out. Now I know she felt judged, and the truth is she was right.

"Even though they had been to marriage counseling, I thought she just hadn't given the marriage enough effort. After all, she was a Christian and God hates divorce. I was embarrassed to admit to my friends that they were splitting up. I was so miserable that I finally got some counseling myself.

"My counselor helped me see how controlling I had always been in Monica's life. Most of the statements I made were *she* statements: 'She upsets me;' 'She should have tried harder.' 'She's selfish.' 'She's always been difficult.' My counselor helped me focus on my own feelings and concentrate on *I* statements: 'I'm upset'; 'I'm embarrassed.' I needed to take responsibility for my own feelings.

"As it turned out, I really didn't understand Monica's situation. I started looking at her as a hurting human being, not just my daughter. As she felt more accepted and understood, she confided to me that her "handsome prince" had been physically abusing her. I learned some painful and deep lessons from that experience. Now I work very hard to come alongside my daughter, but not invade her."

As we accept our children, sometimes we catch a glimpse of the painting God is making. The difficult shadow times give them depth, the day-to-day walks give them form, the successful highlights give them inspiration. Together it makes the picture of our child's journey. Our letting go frees God to paint.

The Circle

The August Steven was eighteen we ran into Shelley and Mickey at freshman orientation at the University of California, Davis. We laughed in surprise and told some old stories about their shared childhood over lunch. Nine years later

Shelley and Mickey drove up to visit me with Shelley's first-born son.

Shelley, wonderfully trim from swimming and glowing from new motherhood, held out her bundle to me. Grand-mother Mickey, talking a mile a minute about the special wonders of this particular baby, kept her eyes focused on the child.

"Can you believe it? Isn't he wonderful? And he's so good. Such a dear boy, aren't you, darling?" she cooed.

As I unzipped three-month-old Christopher's snowsuit and lifted his chubby little body to my lap, my heart turned over. His cheeks were as pink and round as Shelley's had been. A fringe of dark hair framed his small face. I examined the v of his top lip. He looked like a little robin. I counted his tiny fingers, smelled his baby skin, and felt his soft breath against my face. His eyes blinked hard and he smiled. I melted. I fell in love.

I looked up at Mickey. She was looking at me. We both knew what a joy and what a job lay before Shelley. Christopher fussed. I handed him over to Mother, and Shelley snuggled him down next to her breast where he made contented baby sighs and sounds.

As we drank hot tea together, Mickey and I told Shelley of our mothering adventures. We both had grown wiser in the mystery of mothering since our early beginnings. We both had birthed two more children. We retold the tale about Steven biting Shelley. This time we laughed.

I knew this birth changed Shelley's life. Like her mother and me, she will feel the most powerful love in the world. She will experience heartbreaking stress. She will know the joy of being needed. She will feel the exhaustion of the demands. She will experience the profound joy of watching a child grow. She will meet her limitations trying to protect his world. She will laugh. She will cry. She will learn what it is to sacrifice self. She will war with the limits of her own personal freedom. She will have hopes and dreams for her child. She will struggle to give up unrealistic expectations of herself—and Christopher. She will thank God for the gift of his life. She will pray for wisdom and grace to raise him. And in the end she will know what other mothers know—that mothering is one of the most profound and complex human experiences a woman can have.

Thinking It Through

1. Describe what you thought mothering would be like.
2. When did reality hit?
3. Who were your mother role models?
4. How do you want to be like them? How do you want to be different?
5. How do you try to control your child? What is the difference between punishment and discipline?
6. Make a list of the difficult and the wonderful traits of your child. Do you accept the child God has entrusted you to raise, or do you often wish he or she were different?
7. How do you affirm your child's uniqueness?
8. Do you struggle with the perfect mother image? How can you be more realistic and balanced?
9. List your weaknesses as a mother. List your strengths.
10. Can you identify different stages of motherhood? What are some of the challenges of each stage?
11. Are you working to set your child free? What are you doing specifically to help him accomplish his independence?
12. Is your identity wrapped up in mothering? How?
13. What are some unrealistic expectations you hold of your mothering and your children?
14. What are you learning about God from mothering?

"May the Lord make you increase, both you and your children"   *(Ps. 115:14, NIV).*

Chapter Nine

WHO WILL MAKE ME HAPPY?
*Unrealistic Expectations from
the Happiness Myth*

School was out and the days already steamed. I took my calendar off the wall and marked through Monday, June 2, with a red marker. *Only five more days until my birthday. THE BIRTHDAY.* I thought, *Finally I'll be thirteen— a teenager.*

I felt sort of shivery and happy all over. Growing up would be adventure, freedom, and promise. This birthday was the beginning of my REAL growing up.

As I sat leaning against my bunk bed with my arms wrapped around my legs, I began to dream about my day. *I've got to have a real celebration. Something sort of grown-up.* I flipped through a *Seventeen Magazine. If only I could have a dance. A dance at the Yacht Club.* The soft, white, ankle-length dress I saw in the magazine suddenly lifted off the page and on to me. In my mind I floated through family and friends saying, "Thank you for the lovely gifts," and "Yes, thank you! It *is* wonderful to be thirteen." I blinked my eyes hard and turned the page.

The picture showed teenage girls in pastel party dresses standing around a table of tiny sandwiches cut in star shapes. They held cut glass cups of red fruit punch with their pinky fingers sticking out. Now there was a party! A party I could

141

have. A grown-up sort of party. If I could make those fancy sandwiches and mix up that fruit punch and invite my friends, I would have the best party ever. I would be happy for the rest of my life!

And that is exactly what I told my mother.

"Are you sure this is what you want to do?" said Mother. "I thought it might be fun to have a wienie roast at the beach and let Ruth Ann spend the night."

"A wienie roast? That's a little too young," I said, showing her the magazine picture of the sandwiches. "I want to have a birthday tea."

Mother agreed to help me, but I was determined to do the whole thing myself. After all I was going to be thirteen, for goodness sake.

As I planned and prepared my birthday tea, my expectations grew. I would be a wonderful hostess now that I was a teenager. And since we were all growing up, my friends would be impressed by a *real* party—not just some kid thing.

After a fitful night of sleep, my special birthday, June 7, finally arrived. I leaped out of bed. My long, bare feet slapped across the oak wood floor to the bathroom. I put on my glasses and looked into the mirror at my flat chest. No— nothing had happened overnight.

By 7:30 A.M. I was yelling at my little brother, Phil, to clear out of the kitchen. All morning I cut the star shapes out of soft, white bread with a cookie cutter. I spread on the tuna fish and egg salad, topping them off with red-centered olive slices. The day grew hotter and hotter.

"Well, birthday child, you're doing a fine job," said my mother. "If you need any—"

"I don't need a thing. This is the happiest day of my life," I said, as I mixed up the punch and floated the ice chunks on top. I checked the clock. 11:15 A.M. I grabbed the dust rag from under the sink, polished the end tables and stacked the magazines. Sweat trickled down the back of my neck, and my glasses slid down my nose. Time for a bath.

I was ready in my blue and white Sunday dress by 1 o'clock for the 2 o'clock birthday tea. Waiting for my girlfriends to arrive for my party, I paced around like a skinny alley cat. The day was so hot my mother borrowed our neighbor's electric fan. Finally, one by one the girls came. We sat around all dressed up, giggling and sweating together.

"Come on now," I said, carrying around the glass tray. "Have some sandwiches and punch. I fixed it all myself!" The girls nibbled politely at the hard, dried-out stars. Nobody liked tuna fish or egg salad much. The punch had long ago lost its ice and sat warm in the glass Christmas cups. I opened my grown-up presents of body powder and cologne. In an hour the girls left to strip out of their hot dresses. "It was a *wonderful* tea," they all said politely. "Happy Birthday!"

Happy Birthday. Big tears collected underneath the edge of my glasses. Happy Birthday. I threw my dress on the bed and pulled on my shorts. Happy Birthday. I poured the warm red punch down the drain. Happy Birthday. I dumped the dried-up star sandwiches in the garbage. Happy Birthday. I washed the glass Christmas cups. Happy Birthday. I was thirteen and growing up. I would never be happy again!

Expectations of Happiness

Often we think of the ideal state of constantly being happy as the sum of all our expectations. "Don't worry. Be happy." Those words to a recent Grammy award winning song say it all—everyone should be happy. And from an early age we often pinpoint being happy as life's primary goal—the fulfillment of all our expectations. We want to spend our lives in Happiness Land, wallowing in a constant state of bliss.

To find our way to this magic land of milk and honey, we change friends, change schools, change marriage partners, change jobs, change churches, and sometimes even change countries. We read self-help books, seek counseling, and examine our horoscope to find the map to happiness.

We hold unrealistic expectations of parents, friends, authority figures, husbands, children, work, money, even ourselves. We say "If only they would. . . . If only he might. . . . If only I could . . . then I would be happy." These fantasies—these unrealistic expectations—feed the Depression Vulture and rob us of something deeper than happiness. They are the Thief of our joy.

According to *Webster's New Collegiate Dictionary*, the words *happiness* and *haphazard* come from the root word *hap*, which means something that happens or befalls without plan, apparent cause, or predictability. Should we believe that if happy things happen, we succeed and if bad things happen we fail? How can we measure the good of our life based on what "happens" to us?

I believe that God calls us to a deeper land than Happiness Land—a land where "in Him we live and move and have our being" (Acts 17:28, NIV). With Him our losses, our grief, our pain, and our happy times are braided together in a thick, strong, golden strand. We learn to be unafraid because we are walking with our Almighty God. We begin to embrace all of our life. We take up faith. As our own history with God grows, we come to understand that truly, "All things work together for good for them that love God" (Rom. 8:28, KJV).

Mommy, Can You Make Me Happy?

At birth we suffer separation. We enter life and have to breathe, eat, and eliminate on our own. The bliss we knew of total oneness in the womb is gone forever. This separation is only the first of many losses in our young lives having to do with mother.

The totally dependent infant needs the protection of mother and demands constant time, attention, and care. Often, mother can satisfy her with a breast; however, there are times when nothing can quiet her demands. The infant communicates her earache, her stomach pains, her fear by a scream that means "Make me happy! You're my mother!" The mother and child separateness seems profound. And it is.

If we could find complete satisfaction and happiness in our infant stage, we would never begin our painful, natural journey of becoming a separate individual. We need to have the right amount of mother-infant bonding and the right amount of mother-infant separation.

As we move from infant, to toddler, to young child, to adolescent, the task is to let go of mother and separate into our own person. This is tough business. Childhood is never lived out in Happiness Land.

Children who know God find a Holy Partner to love them as they separate and grow. Carol told me about meeting this Love. "When I was a child, my mother used to say, 'These are the happiest days of your life, Carol Ann. Now go and play.'" Carol paused and took a breath. "I was terribly shy. I wanted to stay by my mother. Going out to play with other kids was one of the hardest things I had to do. But I had to do it.

"Leaving Mother's side took great courage—great energy. Especially after my father died the summer I was seven years old. My grandmother came to live with us that summer. I remember she used to rock back and forth in our white cane rocker and sing the old Gospel songs. She let me sit on her lap as long as I wanted. She said God was my heavenly Daddy. He loved me, and I could talk to Him about all my worries.

"'Remember,' she would say, 'He says, "I am with you, and will protect you wherever you go"'" (Gen. 28:15, TLB).

"I believed her. My childhood had happy moments, but I can't say it was happy. I know, though, that out of the times of pain I started my internal journey with One who would never leave me."

Even when we are adults, the child within us may still long for Mother to make things right. A seventy-six-year-old woman recently told me that she was a middle daughter of three girls. "I always wanted Momma to take time to make me happy. She was too worn out I guess." She bent her gray head and whispered, "Sometimes I still dream she might come and tuck me in bed."

Try as we might, we can never fill ourselves with holy nectar from our mothers. It is unreal to believe our mother's job is to keep us happy. Their job is to stand secure and help us complete our separation task so we can become our own person. If we could be totally satisfied by Mother, we would never feel inner thirst. And it is because we *are* thirsty that we learn to come to God and drink.

How thankful we are for the good gift of adequate mother-love. Still, we will never find eternal happiness in Mother. But remember: "When my father and my mother forsake me, then the LORD will take me up" (Ps. 27:10, KJV).

Friends, Please Make Me Happy!

Leaving the safety of home, we venture out looking for connection. We must separate from Mother, but we miss belonging. We miss oneness. We think happiness will flood us when we have a friend to fill our emptiness, but from the beginning we encounter both moments of connection and moments of alienation in friendships.

Growing friendships do shift. When they shift, our relationship becomes uncomfortable. Often, we have unrealistic expectations of friends. They are supposed to be there for us, unchanging, providing the happy security and belongingness we lost from Mother.

Belonging is essential to our well-being. We are happy if we get a lot of valentines from our sixth-grade classmates. We are devastated if we don't. We are happy if we are invited to *the* big party in junior high. We are devastated if we aren't. We all try to look alike, talk alike, and act alike to become one with someone again. Tucked away in our solid group of friends, we will live in Happiness Land forever.

Thirsty to be known and to belong, we manipulate others and give ourselves away in order to have what we want.

Soon we become restless: we are still thirsty.

We long for that Friend who never changes, who will never leave us; the One who will bring us something deeper and more solid than the fleeting moments of happiness.

Friends are my great treasure. Each friend is like a jewel that enriches my life. As I give myself over to friendship and become vulnerable to another, I have learned that friendship has its risks. There is separation in the togetherness. Separation because of miscommunication, disagreement, relocation, death—and sometimes each other's good fortune. If I am to love another person, I must learn to accept our differences in personality and life experience.

As I look for a perfect Friend whose love never fails me, I look into the eyes of Jesus. He tells me, "You are My friends, if you do what I command you" (John 15:14). What He commands me to do is love Him and love others. I can truly love and accept others only because our Lord is loving and accepting me.

My closest friends I call my friends of the right hand. We are servants of Jesus for each other. As Jesus calls us into life, we struggle out of the tomb, as Lazarus did, bound in graveclothes. Then Jesus calls us, as friends, to gently unwrap each other and set each other free.

Christ Jesus is the Great Friend who leads us past Happiness Land into the risky land of growing, profound friendships.

Husband, Won't You Make Me Happy?

Since girlhood we have been waiting to ride on a star in a moon-filled night sky with *him*. With braces on our teeth and pimples on our chins, we embrace our love fantasies and elaborate on them as part of our puberty rites. Surely there will be a Prince Charming to rescue us from abandonment of father and mother. Surely *he* will come to protect us from the world, accept us as we are, and adore us forever.

From our first voice-cracking adolescent boyfriend to the choice of our final prince, we project our fantasies. By manipulating ourselves and him, we work to create the dream of perfect love. The passion of eros gives us the energy. It blinds us, and we are blissfully happy.

But passion cools. Reality strikes. The rent has to be paid. The roof leaks when it rains. She sleeps in curlers and flannel pajamas. He has bad breath and snores. He is a mere man. Her dream is shattered, and she reacts like a mere woman.

"I must be married to the wrong man," she cries. "The deepest longings of my heart and soul are unmet. He doesn't know me, he doesn't understand me, he doesn't love me. He's not a true prince. I'm miserable! I've married an imposter!"

Finding our way through the cutting pieces of a shattered marriage dream means mourning the dream and then giving up unrealistic expectations so we can move on. It means walking deeper into the marriage love by embracing reality. It means seeking for the True Prince who can save, accept, and perfectly love us so we can love our imperfect partners.

The primrose path of marriage we expected turns out to be a rather bumpy, thorny road. If we choose to keep walking with our mates, we can learn deep secrets of communication, forgiveness, and commitment. The colored ribbons of happiness, struggle, pain, success, failure, tears, and laughter weave around the maypole forming a solid picture of what true love looks like.

In the winter of her marriage my grandmother knew more about love than any blushing, springtime bride. Someday the bride will awake in the arms of reality. She too will have to give up impossible expectations of her human husband in order to go on—to risk going deeper in. Giving up the dream is hard. Growing is the reward.

Still, we long for the Perfect Lover.

We must look beyond our husband to satisfy our longings.

If we listen, we will hear Him calling us to be His bride. He says to us, "For your husband is your Maker, whose name is the Lord of hosts; and your Redeemer is the Holy One of Israel, who is called the God of all the earth" (Isa. 54:5).

If we accept His invitation, we will be known. We will belong. We will be loved. We will drink from an eternal spring and be filled. Then we can turn and offer others a cup of cool water.

Our Bridegroom, Jesus, brings us a peace that passes all understanding, but His road doesn't lead us to Happiness Land. Instead, it leads us deep into the challenges of truth, change, and freedom.

Mother Institutions, Won't You Make Me Happy?

As we move into our culture, we look to schools, government agencies, and the church to give us a sense of happy security. We learn early in life that they *owe* us. After all, our parents paid taxes. Now we pay taxes. Also, our grandparents and great grandparents built the city halls, schools, hospitals, and churches of our country. They started the great institutions we inherited.

Marilyn, who worked for the Health, Education, and Welfare Department in Washington, D.C., made this observation: "It seems as if Americans want a big system to take away the sick, the old, the poor, the insane, and the criminals so they won't have to deal with the enemies of their personal pursuit of happiness. This is impossible."

We have unrealistic expectations of American systems. We work to make them work because we are addicted to them. We lean into Mother Institution and look for security, but to get her to work for us, we have to "be nice" and play right. If we learn the rules and play right, she will protect us and we can settle into a safe, happy life.

Mother Institution makes many promises, but when she fouls up, we are left holding the bag. Even though she had altruistic beginnings, in the end Mother Institution often exists only to serve herself.

Of all institutions, the church stands under the most piercing light. On her we place the greatest expectations of all. Within her walls we confess our faith. We are plunged into the cold water of baptism. As we are lifted up, our body breaks through the water into new life. Now at last, here in the church, we will find security and belongingness. Perfect happiness.

But even before we are dry, we find tares growing among the wheat. Disillusioned, some of us turn away when we discover the weak, broken places of the church. Many of us experience a lack of comfort and belonging. We came hungry and we leave hungry. This is true because an institution will never be the source of eternal wholeness and health. Not even the institutional church. Only God Himself can make us whole.

Jesus never said, "Have faith in the institutions. Be happy and let them feed you." He turned the legalist religious system upside down. He said the true church would eat *Him* and be filled. "I am the Bread of Life; he who comes to Me shall not hunger, and he who believes in Me shall never thirst" (John 6:35).

He calls His own to eat from Him, and then to look at the stark reality of the sick, the old, the poor, the insane, and the criminals. He calls us to look and serve as He served. This never takes us to Happiness Land. This takes us on a journey with Him—a journey of both weary grief and great joy.

Things, Work, and Money, Can't You Make Me Happy?

As children, our parents and society teach us to read the highway signs pointing to Happiness Land. One sign in bold red letters reads **THINGS.** Another reads **WORK.** Yet another reads **MONEY.** Wearing blinders like an old mule, some of us plod along until the day we die, following the road signs and hoping to arrive.

"Some people binge on food when they're unhappy," said Peggy. "I binged on work. When I felt threatened, I worked harder and harder. My life was a complicated mess, but I figured when I got what I wanted, I'd be satisfied. You know, content. But I never was."

Peggy went on. "The more power I had, the more I wanted. The more money I made, the more I needed. Then I met Cara. Her attitude about work and life was different from mine. She taught English to immigrants in adult education classes, drove a secondhand car, and rented a cozy but modest apartment. She loved bike riding, movies, good books, camping, her cat, and her friends. She had a commitment to the people she taught. My frantic life paled next to her peace.

"Finally, I asked her to tell me her secret. The secret, she said, was choosing God and a simple life."

People of God need to listen for their calling—their vocation. We must listen and then discipline our gifts and give them to the world.

Christian writer Elizabeth O'Connor understands what this means. In a recent interview with *The Otherside Magazine*, O'Connor says that our true vocation and calling is related to pain, our own pain and the pain of others. True vocation, she explains, has to do with our being healers in the world. If our job doesn't provide this opportunity, we can extend ourselves somewhere else to give our gifts.[1]

Rather than arriving at contented, blissful Happiness Land, we will experience stretching, happy moments by giving away our gifts. Serving others, we will find the struggle of real life and an unfolding, eternal adventure.

Jesus said it is impossible to serve God and mammon, because we would hate the one and love the other. The Pharisees, who were lovers of money, scoffed at Him. I understand the Pharisees for I experience the same driving temptation. I understand their choice, but by choosing mammon we miss what God in Christ wants to give us. Even the happy moments of the power and pleasure of work and money are limited. What folly to stake our hope in the fleeting security of either! Life on earth is too brief.

As much as we treasure a good job and a good income and nice things, choosing God above all else will bring us everlasting security. We should distrust power's guarantee of happiness. Just ask Napoleon. Under holy direction we can joyfully learn to wear the world like a loose garment.

Dear Children, Make Me Happy!

In the dream it is Sunday afternoon after a picnic in the park. The children sit about Mother's feet listening, laughing, loving her—forever. In reality the children go off with friends, leave for the service, college, marriage, or foreign lands. They have picnics with their own children who in turn leave them.

The deep lure of motherhood is to re-create connection, to love someone, yes, but at even a deeper level to be loved by someone. If we control things right, we can try to create everlasting happiness between mother and child.

We find, however, even though we have treasured, happy moments we are out of control. Did our baby forget to bring our ticket to Happiness Land?

If we pick up the cues, baby tells us from her beginning that she is a separate person. She is here to experience life through her own senses, to go through her own seasons. This can be a shock if we expected something different.

Maria calls herself the original Earth Mother. "I loved mothering. I did the whole shot down to the chicken soup for the kids' colds. But I guess I'm what you call a smother-mother. I didn't want to let go.

"When my daughter, Brook, left home at twenty-three, I called her apartment as often as four or five times a day. And I was really hurt if she didn't pay attention to me. Somewhere I had built up a lot of ideas about what she should do to be a good daughter. It was my way of hanging on, but I made myself miserable in the process. I made Brook responsible for my happiness." Maria is learning to let go of Brook and take hold of God. She is learning that her child was never meant to be a vehicle for her total happiness.

Mothering has taught me about my humanity. Through my children I have learned how weak and how strong I am. How consistent and inconsistent. How brave and how frightened. How selfish and how unselfish. How unloving and how loving I can be. I have grown. I am still growing.

Most of all, mothering has thrown me into prayer. As I stumbled along trying to raise my children, I quickly came to the end of myself. Then I learned to ask for holy wisdom and to listen for direction. I prayed for the children's future. I prayed for their present situations. I prayed for their protection. I prayed for their own personal walk with the Holy One. I still pray. I pray and let go.

Mothering weaves her mysterious, ancient story into our lives. We discover, as our mothers and grandmothers discovered, that our job of sitting on our nest of chicks comes to an end. To really love, we must let them fly. Our children can bring us happy moments and also challenge our lives, but never can they be our life. Our life is hid in Christ.

From the beat of America's drum we hear the repeated sounds of "Don't worry, be happy." As we observe life closely, we realize we must move beyond a search for happiness. Our adult task is to mature.

Mature people exhibit wisdom, gentleness, simplicity, love, and peace. They accept happy times and sad times with grace, learning from all aspects of life. As we begin maturing spiritually, we stop trying to suck a happy life from others. Learning to see life through God's eyes changes our focus. We find the deep joy we long for by embracing life and giving our gifts away—from a full place.

Collecting Happy Moments
The sultry air still hung heavy in the early evening of my miserable thirteenth birthday. The humid clouds boiled up

outside, and I boiled up inside thinking about my Birthday Tea. What a flop!

After supper I escaped to my bedroom and stood looking out of the open, narrow window through the blooming gardenia bush. The pungent fragrance flooded my bedroom. Unlatching the window screen, I pushed it open and snapped off a white blossom. I crushed it against my nose. I knew without looking that the gardenia was turning brown from being bruised—like me. What a miserable day!

My father poked his head in the door—without permission. "Barbra Kay, climb in the car," he said. "We're going to the beach to cool off. Come on."

I don't want to go to the beach, I thought. *I just want to stay in my room forever.* Speaking like that to my father would be life-threatening, so I rode in silence the two miles to the beach with my parents and Phil in our old blue Hudson. I was as sullen as the weather.

Flinging the heavy car door open, I climbed down the rough, cement seawall steps to the flat, white beach. The sand held the warmth from the day. It comforted the soles of my bare feet as I made tracks to the water's edge. The calm, warm water splashed at me as I began to run along the shore. The rolling, white foam looked like a ruffle at the bottom of a huge, blue-gray skirt.

The sun dipped past the horizon, leaving its signature of red streaks in the west and the promise of night. The full moon played hide-and-seek with the rolling clouds. When the clouds broke open, the moonshine lit them in silver, made a light path in the water, and illuminated the white sand. What a night! For a long while I danced in the water on the moon-path, prancing like a colt.

"Barbra Kay!" my father shouted across the beach. I galloped back toward him. By the light of a small bonfire, I could see my family crouched around a blanket. My father held a large piece of cardboard to shield something from the breeze.

There in the center of the blanket was a huge green wa-

termelon with thirteen blazing candles. "Hurry," yelled my
brother. "Blow quick." Laughing, I stooped down, made my
wish, and blew. Father took a long knife and cut into the
melon. With a loud crack, it split apart. Instantly, I smelled
the sweet scent of the melon. Father plunged the knife right
into the center and cut a big wedge. "The birthday girl gets
the heart. Tell us how it is!" I filled my mouth with cold
watermelon. Sticky juice ran down my cheeks. "It tastes
great," I said.

"We know you're a teenager," said my mother, "but we
have a present for you. This is to remind you *never* to let the
child deep inside you get too far away." She handed me a
long, narrow package wrapped in Sunday comics and tied
with red string.

"Open it!" said my brother, jumping up and down.
"Open it!" I ripped the paper off. The clouds cleared and
the moonlight lit up my gift—a lemon yellow kite.

"If you take care, you'll have it a long time. It's silk," said
my father. "I've already put the tail on. Take her for a night
flight."

Phil held the kite upright while I stretched the string out
across the beach. "OK. Let her go!" I yelled.

As I sprinted along the beach in the moonlight, the yellow
silk kite soared up with its handsome tail wiggling like a
snake. The clouds and the moon and I played tag. Filled to
the brim with a sense of well-being and the goodness of life,
I was glad God had made me.

I collected the moments of the night and etched them in
my mind: the color of moonlight, the wet of the water, the
warmth of the sand, the sweet taste of the watermelon, the
touch of my family, the flight of my dancing kite. I collected
the memory of these happy moments and stored them inside
me forever.

The night of my thirteenth birthday marks my conscious
collection of happy moments. But it would be years before I
learned how to enjoy the moments as they came instead of
chasing after them. It would be years before I gave up my

quest for Happiness Land and entered into His land of joy. But eventually I changed maps and found my way.

Thinking It Through

1. Is your primary goal to be happy? Where did this happiness goal come from?
2. Do you feel as if you are failing at life if you feel unhappy? Explain.
3. Do you still long for your mother or father to make you happy? How? Do you think of your childhood as being happy or unhappy? Why?
4. Do you feel unhappy if your friends fail to live up to your expectations? List some of the expectations you have of your friends. Are your expectations realistic? Explain.
5. Do you expect your husband to make you happy? What actions are you looking for?
6. What institutions do you depend on? What expectations do you have concerning these systems?
7. How much do you depend on the power of work and money and things to bring you happiness?
8. Do you secretly feel that your children should make you happy? What exactly do you expect them to do or to be to create happiness? Are you being realistic?
9. Do you expect your motherhood role to sustain your happiness? Who is responsible for your emotions?
10. What happy moments have you collected?

"Let them give thanks to the LORD for His unfailing love and His wonderful deeds for men, for He satisfies the thirsty and fills the hungry with good things"

(Ps. 107:8-9, NIV).

Chapter Ten

HOW CAN I LIVE IN JOY?
Realistic Expectations
from Living with God

The early afternoon traffic moved steadily along the 101 freeway as I drove our Ford station wagon to the valley with six-year-old Katie. I took the Fairmont exit. Five more blocks to The Evergreen Convalescent Home.

"How come Grammy's in the hospital?" Katie asked.

"She broke her hip, honey. But she's not in the hospital anymore. Grammy's been moved to a big home where people can help her."

"Is she real sick?"

"Not really. But remember your great-grandmother is ninety-four years old! It's too hard for her to cook and clean or even get dressed now," I said.

"Or even take a bath?"

"Or even take a bath," I answered, nodding my head. My mind flooded with memories of my first meeting with Ethel Heimbaugh after Gary and I married. I remembered her flower beds crowded with masses of bright red geraniums greeting me as I walked up the three cement steps to her front door. Sunshine spilled through the tall, narrow windows of her simple home. English ivy, curly ferns, and pink, white, and purple African violets graced dark oak end tables, the window sills, and a white wicker stand. An antique, black-walnut pump organ dominated the small living room. Grammy's clear, light-blue eyes snapped with intelligence. Her voice tinkled with laughter. She made me feel at home.

After serving us coffee with thick cream and powdered German cookies, she sat her plump, small body at the organ and pumped the pedals vigorously with her tiny feet. Running her arthritic fingers over the keys, she began to sing, "And He walks with me and He talks with me, And He tells me I am His own; And the joy we share as we tarry there, none other has ever known."[1]

"I left Him once." She spoke in a whisper. The sunshine seemed to leave her blue eyes for a moment. "But never again. Never again." Then she laughed and looked straight at me. "Do you love the Lord? In the end there's nothing but the Lord."

"Well, yes. I was raised in the church," I said.

"Not the same thing. Not at all the same thing as *knowing* Him," she said, cocking her white head and smiling as if she held a secret. "Don't stop until you know Him."

Memories of Grammy swirled as I turned into the parking lot, parked, and set the hand brake. It was hard to think of this lively woman totally restricted. I looked at the front door of the drab gray building. My stomach flopped over. I wasn't sure what to expect.

"Come on, honey. You can carry the flowers." I helped my little daughter out of the car with her basket of yellow and white daisies, and we went inside. The receptionist pointed the direction. My shoes clacked like a tap dancer down the shiny, gray linoleum floor through the dark, windowless hall. Katie walked on her tiptoes.

The place smelled like Pine Sol and urine. Men and women sat in steel wheelchairs—some in silence. Some yelling or talking to themselves. Some gentle-faced and waiting. Some like slow old turtles made their way in walkers. Glancing at their faces, I saw the years etched in their skin—and the loneliness. The Depression Vulture's vast shadow seemed to cover the hospital. Everyone here was waiting to die.

I shivered. My palms began to sweat.

"Little girl, little girl. Give me a flower. Come, give me a flower." An ancient lady wrapped in a huge blue shawl cried out and pointed at us. I felt Katie freeze.

"It's OK, Katie," I whispered, plucking out a yellow daisy. "Here you go, dear." I put the thin green stem into the woman's frail hand. Her faded gray eyes teared as she laid the yellow petals against her wrinkled face.

Farther down the gray hall, a tiny, white-haired woman in a pink robe sat bent over like a drooping rose. Her wheelchair faced the wall. I gently touched her shoulder.

"Grammy? Grammy, it's Barbra, Gary's wife—and Katie." Grammy lifted her head. Her blue eyes sparkled.

"So glad you girls are here!" She smiled.

"What are you doing facing the wall?" I asked. My skin felt pinprickly all over. I definitely wanted out of this dark, death-like place.

"Oh, the ladies are fixing my bed," she said cheerfully. "They moved me out of the way. I'm not strong enough to move the chair. So I've been praying. Come on. They're through. You can push me in." Katie held up the flower basket. Grammy reached out her small, gnarled hand and stroked Katie's blond head. I put the basket in Grammy's lap and pushed her into the drab room.

Kleenex, Vaseline, a blue plastic cup, a water pitcher, and four faded daffodils crowded the metal bedside table—along with Grammy's tattered black leather Bible. I threw out the old daffodils and set the basket on the table, nervously arranging the flowers.

"When are you going home, Grammy?" asked Katie.

"I'm not sure, hon. I may stay until I go home to Jesus. He's been building me a mansion, and anytime He's ready for me I'm ready to go." Grammy's tiny lined face began to glow. "He's my true joy, you know." Her thin voice swelled as she spoke through a smile. "And I'm His child."

As I drove the freeway home, I felt weak. *What a horrible*

place. What a horrible state to be in—weak and old and dying. Death's like God's gravel rubbing into our souls to make us pay attention. We really are dust! But how can Grammy be so calm? It's got to be her faith. It's got to be God.

"That hospital's a scary place." Katie's words broke into my thoughts.

"The people are old, honey. Their bodies have worn out."

"Grammy's not scared to die," said Katie.

"You're right. She knows she's going to the Lord," I said, "and she's known for a long time." Satisfied for the moment, Katie lapsed into silence. My mind raced as the miles went under the tires. *How could Grammy, with her mind as sharp as ever, be so cheerful in that place of the dying? How could she be so peaceful? She really lives her faith.* I remembered Grammy's words to me when we first met—words she lived by then and would carry into her new life: "In the end there's nothing but the Lord."

Tears stood in my eyes. I wiped them away with the back of my hand. *Lord, I want to go deeper. I want to drink in more of that holy joy, like Grammy, and live—really live every day.*

The Joy of the Inward Journey

Grammy's life challenged me. She possessed faith and her faith possessed her. She lived it out in simplicity, prayer, study, meditation, and service. She was full of joy. By her own admission her past was riddled with mistakes. But she chose to accept forgiveness and take the deeper road, the inward journey. She challenged me not only to know about Him but to *know* Him. Her words helped to prepare me for my Easter understanding. Jesus is alive. Jesus has risen. He has risen indeed! And I wanted to follow Him.

Those of us who decide to walk with the risen Lord will finally experience true joy. We come to understand, like the saints before us, that "Man's chief end is to glorify God and enjoy Him forever."[2]

As we establish our life in the Lord, we practice drawing our life from His life. Through Christian disciplines, we experience life with our Lord. As we grow to know Him, we learn we can always have joy and peace—not because we perfect ourselves or our circumstances but because of who *He* is.

Paul tells us, "Rejoice always" (1 Thes. 5:16) and "Rejoice in the Lord always; again I will say, rejoice!" (Phil. 4:4). The Hebrew word we translate as rejoice actually means "return to the source of our joy." By returning to the source of our joy, the troubles of life no longer rape us. We face them. We grieve. We grow. And all the while we can have joy in Him because of His love for us (Eph. 3:14-21).

If we can take joy in Him, we can find that peace that passes human understanding. Our deep emptiness will be filled up with God. No longer will we try to fill our unrelenting needs through parents, friends, lovers, husbands, children, jobs, money, things, organizations, or even ourselves.

Leaning into Him, we can begin to let go of control—to accept the give and take of life and to forgive. As we let go of our joy robber, the unrealistic expectations we have fostered, we will find new freedom. We can accept our identity in Christ Jesus. We are the child who was longed for. We are the person who is accepted. We are the woman who is cherished. We can always rejoice in the One who promises, "Lo, I am with you always" (Matt. 28:20).

Beginning the Walk

The deeper walk seems like a path for angels, praying holy women, and empowered ministers. How could I, an ordinary woman, who washes dishes, wipes little noses, drives carpools, and teaches school, develop a different and deep spiritual lifestyle? My feet are too dirty to step on such holy ground. Yet, I yearn to follow Him.

One October evening after dinner, I wrapped up in my old beige trench coat and slipped out of the house to take a walk. My friend Alice would meet me at the corner. The sounds of the day rattled in my head as I took long strides down the sidewalk. The damp smells of fall filled the night. Crisp dead leaves crunched and broke to pieces under my tennis shoes. Hanging on the trees, red and yellow leaves waited to drop because it was their time.

My life is so short, I thought. *Soon it will be my time to go back to dust. I'm not as secure as Grammy about dying. I feel afraid. I know how the play ends but I don't know all my lines. My last earth scene—my own dying scene—scares me. I know I belong to the Lord. I know I'll end up with Him. But how am I going to live while I still have life?* A gust of fall wind rushed against me. More leaves lifted off the trees, floated like tiny air boats, and settled in piles on the ground.

I turned the corner. Alice lifted her hand in a wave and a grin spread across her freckled face. Her red hair poked out in little tufts around the hood of her white jacket. She still looked refreshingly childlike in her mid-fifties.

"Why so glum?" She caught my mood and picked up my stride. She walked along in quiet, waiting for me to explain.

"I've just been thinking."

Alice laughed. "OK, what's going on?" She was used to me. Our friendship centered around questions.

"Life's really short. The older I get, the faster time goes, and I just want to make it count. You seem so deep in your faith and full of joy. How do you walk with God?"

Alice walked in silence. Then she said, "I guess I started long ago by making friends with Him." She took my arm and pulled me to a stop. "Barbra, making friends with some- one takes time. Spend time with Him. Get to know Him."

Alice's words encouraged me. Perhaps if I got to know God, I might discover who He is, not who I *think* He is.

Getting to know God is the open secret A.W. Tozer writes about in his book *The Knowledge of the Holy*. It is knowing Him that brings us to the deeper walk.

I bring no esoteric cryptogram, no mystic code to be painfully deciphered. I appeal to no hidden law of the unconscious, no occult knowledge meant only for a few. The secret is an open one which the wayfaring man may read. It is simply the old and ever-new counsel: *Acquaint thyself with God.*[3]

The Gift of Time

The first order of business is to spend time with our Holy Friend. After all, He gave time to us to begin with. In our decision to be with Him, we offer the gift of ourselves. Going to church on Sunday will not provide enough time with Him for people desiring His joy. We need more than daily fifteen-minute Bible study and prayer to sustain joy.

Living with Him is another mind-set all together. Living with Him means *being* with Him moment by moment. It means, instead of talking to ourselves, we learn to talk with Him—about everything. By being with Him, we learn about our Beloved. And knowing Him, we rejoice!

To engage in this moment by moment lifestyle you must ask—do I *want* the abundant life? If you do, then practice the discipline of intimate living by spending *all* your time with your Creator. It is this life, rich with joy, which is hidden in each moment with Him.

Spending our moments with God does take practice, but it is the key to a changed life. Brother Lawrence, who at fifty-five became a Lay Brother with the Carmelites in 1666, wrote about practicing the presence of God:

> In order to first form the habit of conversing with God continually and of referring all that we do to Him, we must first apply ourselves to Him with diligence. After a little such care we shall find His love inwardly excites us to His presence without any difficulty.[4]

Frank Laubach, great missionary, writer, and educator, wrote in 1930, "We shall not become like Christ until we give Him more time."[5]

Giving Him our minds while we go through our everyday activities, seems difficult in the beginning. But it is like having our most beloved friend with us no matter what we are doing. Loving us, guiding us, celebrating, laughing, and crying with us—this is what the deep journey is about.

Once we are accepted by the Father through Jesus, we are not to flop down into the feather bed of grace and expect God's joy to splash over us forever. Discipleship is more than being special pets of the Father.

We are His children and we need training. He calls us to spend time with Him. He calls us to walk with Him. Walk is action. That means we do something. By the doing, by practicing the Way, we change from the inside out.

In *The Spirit of the Disciplines* Dallas Willard writes:

No one ever says, "If you want to be a great athlete, go vault eighteen feet, run the mile under four minutes," or, "If you want to be a great musician, play Beethoven's violin concerto." Instead, we advise the young artist or athlete to enter a certain kind of overall life, one involving deep associations with qualified people as well as rigorously scheduled time, diet, and activity for the mind and body.

But what would we tell someone who aspired to live well in general? If we are wise, we would tell them to approach life with the same general strategy. So, if we wish to follow Christ—and to walk in the easy yoke with Him—we will have to accept His overall way of life as our way of life *totally*. Then and only then, we may reasonably expect to know by experience how easy is the yoke and how light the burden.

The secret of the easy yoke, then, is to learn from Christ how to live our total lives, how to invest all our time and our energies of mind and body as He did.[6]

How do we learn from Christ? By spending time with Him.

I love to visit Martha because Martha lives with God, so I hurry up the long sidewalk through the immense green lawn in order not to waste the precious moments. I see her coming. Her light, short hair surrounds her head like a halo. Light radiates from her seventy-six-year-old face. Tall and straight and slender, she walks regally through the lobby of the retirement home where she lives, touching the people with a word, a pat, or a smile as she goes by.

She looks as if nothing difficult has ever touched her life. But she has had her share of life's suffering. Even now she is losing her brilliant companion of fifty-four years. Her husband, Peter, clouded over with the ravages of Alzheimer's disease, must live in a care unit.

Martha's joy amazes me, and today at lunch I ask her, "How do you stay so joyful? What's your secret? It can't be easy, especially with Peter." She lays her fork down on her salad plate and wipes her long, elegant fingers on her blue napkin, obviously taking her time before she speaks.

"First of all I know who I worship. His promises to me are absolute, so I trust Him. My joy is a permanent resting place in the Lord. That's the best way I can describe it. A knowing, really, rather than an emotional feeling." She breaks open her roll and butters it.

"How did you get to that place of knowing?" I was looking for a secret word from her that would charge up my spiritual life.

"I spend time with my Beloved. And I practice the disciplines of the faith." She looks into my face and winks. "You already know what those are, don't you?"

"Yes, if you mean Bible study, meditation, and prayer. But I have to be honest. Sometimes that gets a little dry."

"Never mind that. A disciple keeps the disciplines. You can use your imagination to change the flow of things. But the inner disciplines change us from the inside. We become remade. The change shows up in outer disciplines of our life like living in simplicity and service—not because we have to but because being re-created—we *want* to."

I leave Martha challenged once again. I can see that the disciplines are the way we give the Lord time—so we can be changed by His presence.

In *The Gift of Time* William T. McConnell writes:

> It may seem simplistic, even mystical, to propose that our hope lies in our devotional life. But if, as C.S. Lewis so aptly illustrates in *The Great Divorce*, if the gates of hell are bolted from the inside, then only an inner transformation can meet the purpose. God's re-creation begins within our inner time, releasing the pressure on the mainspring of our lives. With eternity in our hearts, there is no need to be harassed in our schedules. "In repentance and rest is your salvation, in quietness and trust is your strength" (Isa. 30:15). . . . Time spent with the Beloved means something altogether different from time spent with the rest of the crowd."[7]

The Call of the Crowd

On my drive back home I thought about Martha's words. They frustrated me. My schedule was packed to the brim with work, children, meetings. The only way I could see Martha was to squeeze out the time after my doctor's appointment. Maybe she'd forgotten how life scrambles together when you're raising a family and also trying to work.

No, that wasn't it. Martha had always carried a tremendous schedule. Even now she speaks at Bible conferences, leads retreats, helps care for her husband every day, and counsels and loves those around her.

I knew what she was telling me. In the common things, in the everyday moments, I could live with Him. And the disciplines could give me support and direction for purposeful times of focus.

If I really wanted to experience love and transformation, I had to pursue the excellent Way. It wasn't going to be easy. Now Paul's words made sense to me:

I do not consider myself yet to have taken hold of it. But one thing I do: Forgetting what is behind and straining toward what is ahead, I press on toward the goal to win the prize for which God has called me heavenward in Christ Jesus (Phil. 3:13-14, NIV).

I felt a rush of excitement. I understood. No one becomes an excellent singer, writer, surgeon, runner, or painter without practice, study, or discipline. To become a deep-walker, enjoying Him, would mean personal discipline. I had the finest teacher and coach to encourage me. The Holy Spirit!

No, spiritual depth will never come by osmosis from another person or applying one quick secret. Shortcuts to the inner life are out. Like all other pilgrims I have to make this journey to the Source myself. In spite of the rush of the crowd. Yes, in the midst of the rush of the crowd.

Time for God

One of the greatest challenges in spending time with God is fighting the pressures of the urgent. Often we give our time and self away to whomever or whatever makes the most noise. The nagging urgent is rarely the most important. The pressures frequently come from unrealistic demands of our society or ourselves.

We must stop and think and decide what is our goal. Then we can choose the important over the urgent. By working on the issue of time, we begin to sense the difference between the rushing earth-clock and our soul's eternal-clock. If we have chosen a life of joy with God, we must give Him priority time. We can live our days in excellence.

In an oblong gold frame on the wall above the phone in my childhood home hangs a poem—teaching me as long as I can remember.

Look to this day
For every yesterday is only a dream

And tomorrow is only a vision
But today, well lived
Makes every yesterday a dream of happiness
And every tomorrow a vision of hope
Look to this day, therefore,
For such is the salutation of the dawn.[8]

It reminds me to live each moment well—with God.

The Beautiful Disciplines

There is no *easy* way into the deep walk of freedom. But the yoke is light. The steps to the deeper life may not come in this order to each individual, but they come.

● We realize God is calling us to a life deeper than "church going."

● We realize this new life takes quality time.

● We realize we can learn about God from His Word and His true believers.

● We realize to walk the more excellent Way takes practice.

● We realize we can grow by practicing the disciplines.

● We realize that through time, discipline, and patience we will come to know our God.

● We realize God wants to be known and sends His own Spirit to help us.

● We realize, knowing God, that we will glorify Him and enjoy Him forever.

Most of us have unrealistic expectations of God. He is a mixture of American culture, myth, and leftover father figures. We view Him as a combination of cosmic boss man, Santa Claus, benevolent king, and powerful general. We could never be accepted and loved by a God like that.

To find out about our eternal, unchanging God, we must stay in the Word, live in His presence, communicate with Him, and live with His people. We must throw out our stereotypical god and let God be Himself.

God is not who we *think* He is. He is who He is. The great I AM. How wonderful to know that we will explore Him for an eternity and never come to the end of knowing Him! It is our exploration, our being with Him that begins to change our inner being. We are unafraid to see ourselves in the presence of such love. We stop rationalizing, hiding, or pretending. We release our lives to Him. We are renewed.

Spiritual disciplines are exercises—activities to ready us to take in more of His life for use in the kingdom. In *The Spirit of the Disciplines*, Willard highlights some of the disciplines we can choose from:

Disciplines of Abstinence
   solitude
   silence
   fasting
   frugality
   chastity
   secrecy
   sacrifice
Disciplines of Engagement
   study
   worship
   celebration
   service
   prayer
   fellowship
   confession
   submission[9]

We do not drape ourselves with these disciplines like heavy chains. Rather, we approach the disciplines with excitement, trying a few at a time. They are for spiritual discovery. They are like wearing a gleaming string of pearls.

Regard these and other disciplines with imagination and freshness. Make up your own list. Have a close fellow believer give you a discipline. I am working on living in truth, so I was recently given the discipline for a month to refrain from making exaggerated remarks.

The idea is to learn who our God is and to participate with Him. The *activities* don't change us. Rather, they open our inner self. Then God uses the disciplines as a vehicle to reveal Himself—and grow us up and into Him.

Being with Him, practicing the more excellent way, we begin to know God. The great I AM. Truth. Wisdom. Mercy. Love. Judge. King. Creator. Unchanging. Majestic. Eternal. Good. Holy. Perfect. We come to trust. We come to peace. We come to the Source of joy.

We hear Paul when he writes:

Finally, brethren, whatever is true, whatever is honorable, whatever is right, whatever is pure, whatever is lovely, whatever is of good repute, if there is any excellence and if anything worthy of praise, let your mind dwell on these things.

The things which you have learned and received and heard and seen in me, practice these things; and the God of peace shall be with you (Phil. 4:8-9).

This is the discipline of the faith.

Freedom from the Thief

On the Saturday before Christmas, the presents are stuffed in my closet in paper sacks and boxes wait to be wrapped. Abandoned Christmas cards sit in stacks beside the address book in the den. Cookbooks and stained recipe cards string out across the kitchen counter. The pungent scent of pine reminds me I should finish putting the shiny bobbles, strings of lights, homemade ornaments, and our angel on the tree.

I glance at the list of "to-do's" stuck under the yellow magnet on the refrigerator and sigh. *I want everything perfect. Let's see. Katie's coming home from college tomorrow night, her boyfriend, Tuesday. I've got to make sure the hide-a-bed isn't full of surprises for him. Jeff's to be home Thursday, and Steve and Kathy on Friday.* I smile thinking of my new daughter-in-law and frown thinking of the press of time and undone chores. A weight settles on my chest. I feel my middle-aged body sag.

The back door slams. "Come with me to the beach." My husband's voice slices through my tight thoughts. "There's a negative tide this afternoon. Perfect day for abalone. We've got to hurry to make it. Come on!"

I look around at the Christmas confusion and open my mouth to complain and protest. But I feel His nudge. *Go.*

As Gary and I drive along in our old, blue Volvo filled with black wet suits, buckets, towels, and jackets, my mind stews over my list. Perched beside me, his talons gripping the edge of the front seat, is that old Depression Vulture. He begins pecking at my brain. "What are you doing, going off to the beach?" he hisses. "You *should* be writing those cards. What about poor sick Mrs. Thomas? You *should* go visit. When are you going to bake? You *should* get everything done and make everyone happy!"

That horrible Thief of unrealistic expectations comes with familiar haunts, trying to steal my joy. The old "if onlys" and "what ifs" stir up to take over my thoughts and demand time.

After working on this for years, I recognize the Thief. I laugh, reminding myself to let go and live in the moment.

I focus beyond the windshield to the world rushing by. The day, dazzling with bright winter sun, makes me feel alive. *Lord, this day's incredible. And I almost missed it.* Miraculously, the Depression Vulture vanished.

We park on a rocky cliff high above the beach. I zip up my old, blue down jacket against the nippy sea wind, rub my face with sunblock, and tie on my broken-down panama hat with a wide scarf. Gary struggles into his tight wet suit and together we make our way down the steep cliff to the edge of the water. The tide is way out.

"Good luck," I shout as he hurries down to the right and disappears around the rocks with his gear.

I am alone. I lick my dry lips and taste the salt as I walk down the beach. My tennis shoes make a slight slurping sound as they press into the wet sand. As far as I can see there is endless blue-gray ocean reflecting choppy pieces of bright light. The sky is egg-shell blue. Through the artistry of the wind, fat white clouds magically change shape and cast giant, playful shadows on the Pacific Ocean.

I listen to the soft sound of waves rolling in. White and gray sea gulls caw, lift up from the rocks, and skim along the water searching for dinner. Silhouetted against the sun, a pair of brown pelicans suddenly fold their wings, dive straight down into the water, and come up with a catch.

Everything is filled to the brim with life. Oh, my God. I love You! Now, I taste the salt from my own tears. *I want to be alive—and in love like You made me to be.*

Stooping down, I peer into the tide pools teeming with mysterious creatures. Light purple, pink, yellow, and green sea anemones wave their flowerlike tentacles. Spiny sea urchins look like tiny water porcupines. I stick my fingers in the cold water to move away some thick, golden brown seaweed, and I find a large, white sand dollar. Small hermit crabs scurry into crevices as I stir the pool with a stick. I slip. The toe of my shoe dips underwater. My foot soaked, I shiver from the cold.

Standing to leave, I see in another tide pool a large, leathery, reddish-brown starfish. I climb around to look. It has lost one of its five arms. I know that if a starfish's arm is injured or threatened, it drops off and another arm grows. But it can't regenerate without its central disc.

I had never actually seen this before. I look closer. Sure enough, a new fifth arm was beginning to grow. I begin smiling. *Why, I'm like this starfish. When I stay centered, I drop off the old me, and I am remade.*

Out of the silence of my stillness come deep, quiet words:

You are My creation and My re-creation.
You are My child.

My daughter, drink from Me and
be full of My joy!

I feel like dancing. I feel like singing. I feel like kneeling.
One more time I am reaching up to Him to find Him reaching down to me.

Once again He fills me with Himself.

Thinking It Through

1. Do you long for a deeper spiritual life? Describe what a deep spiritual life means to you.
2. Who are your spiritual role models? Why?
3. How would you personally describe God? Where did your ideas of God come from?
4. What does having a friendship with God mean to you? List the ways you can establish and strengthen a friendship with God.
5. How much time do you spend with God? Write about your experiment of moment by moment living with Him.
6. When you focus on the reality of God loving you, do you experience joy? What does joy feel like to you?
7. What disciplines have you experienced? What disciplines not listed can you think of that might help you deepen your spiritual walk?
8. Who are the spiritual people in your life you can bond with for prayer, discernment, and encouragement?
9. Do you think of walking with God as a heavy or a light yoke? Explain.
10. Do you feel that your chief aim is to glorify God and enjoy Him forever? How will you do this?
11. What happens in your life when you let God love you?

"These things I have spoken to you, that My joy may be in you, and that your joy may be made full"

(John 15:11).

Notes

Chapter 2

1. Bruce Narramore, *Help! I'm a Parent* (Grand Rapids, Michigan: Zondervan Publishing House, 1972), p. 13.
2. "What Every Child Needs for Good Mental Health," National Association for Mental Health, Inc., Rosslyn, Virginia.
3. Martin E.P. Seligman, *Helplessness* (San Francisco: W.H. Freeman and Co., 1975), pp. 178–184.
4. M. Scott Peck, M.D., *The Road Less Traveled* (New York: Simon and Schuster, 1978), p. 85.
5. W. Hugh Missildine, M.D., *Your Inner Child of the Past* (New York: Simon and Schuster, 1963).
6. Lewis B. Smedes, *Forgive and Forget: Healing the Hurts We Don't Deserve* (New York: Harper and Row, 1984), p. 1.

Chapter 3

1. Anne Wilson Schaef, *Co-Dependence: Misunderstood-Mistreated* (Minneapolis: Winston Press, Inc., 1986), p. 44.
2. M. Scott Peck, M.D., *The Road Less Traveled* (New York: Simon and Schuster, 1978), p. 99.
3. Dr. Alan Loy McGinnis, *The Friendship Factor* (Minne-

apolis: Augsburg Publishing House, 1979), pp. 26, 39, 50, 58, 81, 92, 102, 108, 110, 126.

Chapter 4

1. "Doctor Dobson Answers Your Questions," *Focus on the Family*, November 1988, p. 7.
2. Jeannine Stein, "The $1500 Prom Night," *Los Angeles Times*, Thursday, June 2, 1988, p. 1.
3. Anne Wilson Schaef, *When Society Becomes an Addict* (San Francisco: Harper and Row, 1987) p. 68.
4. "News and Stuff," *Focus on the Family*, November 1987, p. 11.
5. Alvin P. Sanoff, "Human Intelligence Isn't What We Think It Is," *U.S. News and World Report*, March 19, 1984, p. 75.
6. Douglas R. Groothuis, *Unmasking the New Age* (Downers Grove, Illinois: InterVarsity Press, 1986), p. 19.

Chapter 5

1. Richard Foster, *Money, Sex and Power: The Challenge of the Disciplined Life* (New York: Harper & Row, 1985), p. 182.
2. "A 51-Gun Salute to Everyday Heroes," *Newsweek*, July 6, 1987, p. 62.
3. *Radix Magazine, Inc.*, Berkeley, California: Vol. 19 No. 1, p. 9.
4. Paul Tournier, *The Healing of Persons* (San Francisco: Harper and Row, 1965), preface, xiii.
5. Dr. Bernie Siegel, M.D., *Love, Medicine, and Miracles* (New York: Harper and Row, Publishers, 1988), p. 19.
6. Cathy Guisewite, "Cathy," *Los Angeles Times*, July 21, 1988.
7. "A 51-Gun Salute to Everyday Heroes," p. 62.
8. Sharon Gallagher, "Interview with Madeleine L'Engle," *Radix*, Vol. 18. No. 3, p. 12.
9. Foster, *Money, Sex and Power*, p. 243.

Chapter 6
1. David Augsburger, M.D., *When Enough Is Enough* (Ventura, California: Regal Books, 1984), p. 66.
2. M. Scott Peck, M.D., *The Road Less Traveled* (New York: Simon and Schuster, 1978), p. 88.
3. Augsburger, *When Enough Is Enough*, p. 82.
4. Anne Herring, Album *To the Bride*, Barry McGuire, 2nd Chapter of Acts, "A Band Called David," Waco, Texas: Myrrh, Word, Inc., 1975: copyright, Latter Rain Music. 1975.

Chapter 7
1. Richard J. Foster, *Money, Sex and Power: The Challenge of the Disciplined Life* (New York: Harper and Row, 1985), p. 44.
2. Richard J. Foster, *Celebration of Discipline* (New York: Harper and Row, Publishers, 1978), pp. 78–83.
3. Oswald Chambers, *My Utmost for His Highest* (New York: Dodd, Mead & Company, 1935), p. 142.

Chapter 8
1. Louis Genevie, Ph.D., and Eva Margolies, *The Motherhood Report: How Women Feel about Being Mothers* (New York: McGraw-Hill, 1987), p. 4.
2. Dr. T. Berry Brazelton, "Working Parents," *Newsweek*, February 13, 1989, p. 66.
3. Ibid., p. 70.
4. Genevie, Margolies, *The Motherhood Report*, p. 206.
5. Barbra Minar, *Children in Crisis/Parents in Pain*, Solvang, California, 1986.

Chapter 9
1. Elizabeth O'Connor, "Faces of Faith," *The Otherside Magazine*, Jan/Feb, 1989, pp. 17–21.

Chapter 10
1. C. Austin Miles, "In the Garden," Copyright 1912, Hall-Mack Company.

2. Westminster Confession of Faith, Shorter Catechism 1st Part.

3. A.W. Tozer, *The Knowledge of the Holy* (New York: Harper and Row Publishers, 1961), p. 121.

4. Frank Laubach and Brother Lawrence, *Practicing His Presence* (Goleta, California: Christian Books, 1973), p. 54.

5. Ibid., p. 35.

6. Dallas Willard, *The Spirit of the Disciplines* (San Francisco: Harper and Row, 1988), pp. 8–9.

7. William T. McConnell, *The Gift of Time* (Downers Grove, Illinois: InterVarsity Press, 1983), p. 20.

8. Anonymous, "Salutation to the Dawn."

9. Dallas Willard, *The Spirit of the Disciplines*, p. 158.

Books for Believers

Bonhoeffer, Dietrich. *Life Together*. San Francisco: Harper and Row, Publishers, 1954.

Chambers, Oswald. *My Utmost for His Highest*. New York: Dodd, Mead & Company, 1935.

Christianson, Evelyn. *Lord, Change Me*. Wheaton, Illinois: Victor Books, 1978.

Colson, Charles. *Born Again*. Old Tappan, New Jersey: Chosen Books, 1976.

Duckworth, Marion. *The Strong Place*. Wheaton, Illinois: Tyndale House, 1983.

Foster, Richard J. *Celebration of Discipline*. San Francisco: Harper and Row, 1978.

Foster, Richard J. *Freedom of Simplicity*. San Francisco: Harper and Row, 1981.

God Calling. Edited by A.W. Russell, Old Tappan, New Jersey: Jove Publications, Inc., 1982.

Hurnard, Hannah. *Hind's Feet on High Places*. Old Tappan, New Jersey: Spire Books, Fleming H. Revell Co., 1973.

Jones, Alan W. *Journey Into Christ*. New York: The Seabury Press, 1977.

Kelly, Thomas R. *A Testament of Devotion*. New York: Harper and Row, 1981.

Kempis, Thomas à. *The Imitation of Christ.* Milwaukee: Bruce Publishing Co., 1940.

Laubach, Frank and Brother Lawrence. *The Practice of the Presence of God.* Goleta, California: Christian Books, 1973.

L'Engle, Madeleine. *Walking on Water.* New York: Bantam Books, 1980.

Letter of the Scattered Brotherhood. Edited by Mary Strong. New York: Harper and Row, 1948.

Lewis, C.S. *Mere Christianity.* New York: Macmillan Publishing Company, 1943.

Lewis, C.S. *The Great Divorce.* New York: Macmillan Publishing Company, 1947.

Lewis, C.S. *The Chronicles of Narnia.* New York: Macmillan Publishing Company, 1954.

Lindbergh, Anne Morrow. *Gifts From the Sea.* New York: Pantheon Books, 1975.

Marshall, Catherine. *Beyond Ourselves.* New York: Avon Books, 1968.

Muggeridge, Malcolm. *A Third Testament.* New York: Ballantine Books, 1976.

Murray, Andrew. *Abide in Christ.* Springdale, Pennsylvania: Whitaker House, 1979.

Nouwen, Henri J.M. *The Way of the Heart.* New York: Ballantine Books, 1981.

Packer, J.I. *Knowing God.* Downers Grove, Illinois: InterVarsity Press, 1973.

Peck, M. Scott. *The Road Less Traveled.* New York: Simon and Schuster, 1978.

Richardson, Don. *The Peace Child.* Glendale, California: Regal Books, 1974.

Schaeffer, Frances. *True Spirituality.* Wheaton, Illinois: Tyndale House Publishers, 1971.

Smith, Hannah Whitall. *The Christian's Secret of a Happy Life.* Old Tappan, New Jersey: Jove Publications, Inc., 1983.

Solzhenitsyn, Alexander I. *The Gulag Archipelago.* New York: Harper and Row, 1973.

Webbe, Gale D. *The Night and Nothing.* San Francisco:

Harper and Row, 1964.
Willard, Dallas. *The Spirit of the Disciplines*. San Francisco: Harper and Row, 1988.
Willard, Dallas. *In Search of Guidance*. Ventura, California: Regal Books, 1984.